Japan

Cheap
& Easy

Japan

Cheap & Easy

A Practical Guide
to Daily Life in
Japan

J. Robert Magee

WEATHERHILL
New York • Tokyo

First edition, 1993
First Weatherhill edition, 1998

Published by Weatherhill, Inc.
568 Broadway, Suite 705
New York, NY 10012

First published by Yohan Publications, Inc., Tokyo, Japan

Planned and edited by SOA Communications Co. Ltd.
Illustrated by Masumi Kamiyama. Cover design by D.S. Noble.

Library of Congress Cataloging-in-Publication Data

    Magee, J. Robert.
        Japan cheap and easy: a practical guide to daily life in Japan /
    by J. Robert Magee. —1st Weatherhill ed.
            p.   cm.
        Originally published: Tokyo: Yohan Pub., 1993.
        ISBN 0-8348-0422-0
        1. Japan—Guidebooks.   I. Title
    DS805.2.M25 1998
    915.204'49—dc21   97-51892
                                                                  CIP

Contents

1 Emergencies, Health and Missing Items

Emergencies

You don't need to be fluent in Japanese and you don't need a translator. You can get emergency help anywhere in Japan if you remember the information on these pages.

TO CALL AN AMBULANCE, DIAL 119
TO REPORT A FIRE, DIAL 119
TO REPORT A CRIME OR TRAFFIC ACCIDENT, CALL 110

You can expect the operator to ask for your name and the site of the emergency. The person who answers the line may or may not speak fluent English, but if you speak slowly, calmly and clearly, you can get the help you need.

At most payphones you don't need any money to contact emergency units. Just pick up the receiver and push the red emergency button, and you'll be connected with an operator. However, pink and red payphones are not equipped with this service, and the 119/110 numbers don't work either (you can hear the operators, but they can't hear you), so avoid those phones and ask someone to help you.

Ambulance Service

The nationwide response time for an ambulance in Japan is around six and a half minutes, which is reassuring, as ambulance staff are not allowed to administer first aid. Their job is to keep you alive until they get you to the nearest hospital, nothing else. To this end, they will give you oxygen and artificial respiration, but that's it.

It speeds up admission to a hospital if you have your insurance papers with you (see p. 14-19).

Ambulance service is supported by your resident's tax, so you pay nothing when you use the service.

Hospitals (General Information)   03-3212-2323

The Fire Department

Fires were particularly devastating in the days when Japanese houses were constructed largely of wood and paper. Building materials have changed and fire departments have improved, but fires can still cause a lot of damage in a city with so many people packed so tightly together.

The same 119 that gets you ambulance service will also get you the fire department. Like ambulances, fire units will come to your aid faster if you can tell the emergency operator exactly where you are. It's a very good idea to know your address in Japanese, and even better if you can give specific directions to your house or apartment. ("I am in the BBB building, next to MMM elementary school.")

The Police Department

If you need the police in an emergency situation, call 110 or push the emergency button on a payphone. As when reporting other emergencies, you should keep calm and give the operator basic details like your name and location.

In addition to emergency situations, you are required to call the police if you are involved in any sort of traffic accident, even if no one is hurt and there are no damages. If you are in an accident and fail to notify the police, you can be arrested as a hit-and-run offender.

Though you should have your Alien Registration Certificate with you at all times anyway, be positively sure you have it with you when you have any dealings with the police. You must be able to produce it on demand. (see p. 24-26).

Police (General Information)   03-3501-0110

Useful Words and Phrases

These words and expressions can help you when reporting emergencies:

My name is...	*Namae wa ... desu*
My address is ...	*Juusho wa ... desu*
I'm at ...	*... ni imasu*
... near (SSS station)	*(SSS eki) no chikaku desu*
Help me	*Tasukete*
Please come quickly	*Sugu kite kudasai*
Ambulance	*Kyuukyuusha*
Please call an ambulance	*Kyuukyuusha o yonde kudasai*
I need an ambulance	*Kyuukyuusha o onegai shimasu*

Please call the fire department	*Shoubousha o yonde kudasai*
The Police/Policeman	*Keisatsu/Omawari-san*
Please call a policeman	*Omawari-san o yonde kudasai*

There's been an accident	*Jiko desu*
There's a fire	*Kaji desu*
There's a thief	*Dorobou desu*
My ... has been stolen	*Watashi wa ... o nusumareta*

Wallet/billfold	*Saifu*
Suitcase	*Suutsukeisu*
Bag	*Baggu*
Bicycle	*Jitensha*

For most other emergencies it may be better for you to ask "please come quickly", then explain things when the authorities arrive.

What Should I Do During an Earthquake or a Major Fire?

You know that Japan is a land of earthquakes. Combine that knowledge with the fact that there hasn't been much progress in the field of earthquake prevention and you'll realize that the best thing you can do is to prepare for the worst before it happens.

Fortunately, most of Japan's earthquakes are of low intensity. Lights sway to and fro and the earth trembles for a bit, but everything quickly returns to normal.

The Great Kanto Earthquake of 1923 is an example of just how much damage a major quake can do, but a large part of the damage resulted from fires that spread across Tokyo after the quake. The quake struck just before lunchtime, which meant homes and restaurants across the region had their charcoal stoves and ovens going full-blaze. It brought wood and paper roofs and walls down on top of burning stoves and a large part of Tokyo was in flames before anyone knew what had happened.

Charcoal has long since been replaced as Japan's main fuel for heating and cooking, and today's buildings are far more fire-resistant than they were 70 years ago, but the threat of fire after an earthquake is still very real.

Follow the steps below when an earthquake occurs.

1) Extinguish all fires, heaters and other sources of fire at once.
2) If a small fire starts, extinguish it immediately.
3) Open a door or window to make sure you have a way out.
4) Get under a strong table, a doorway, a place where roof beams meet, or a similar place where you will be safe from falling objects.
5) Do not run outside.

After the quake stops, listen for information on the radio, or listen to loudspeaker broadcasts from the authorities.

Disaster relief officials recommend that you have enough food and water on hand for at least three days. Other suggested items include a transistor radio, matches, a flashlight, and first-aid materials.

Pre-earthquake preparations can reduce damage caused by a major quake and can make cleaning up afterwards a lot easier. Avoid putting things on the tops of tall cabinets and other places from which they can easily fall. You can buy clasps and straps in your local department stores to keep refrigerators and cabinets upright. Make sure you have some sort of fire extinguisher in your house.

In the event of a major fire after an earthquake, go to your city or ward evacuation areas. These are usually located in large parks, near schools, or beside rivers, but check with your city or ward office to make sure. Many city and ward offices have disaster/earthquake preparedness information in English.

Health Insurance

Insurance and Medical Care in Japan

Japanese medical facilities operate on the premise that everyone has health insurance. The strength of insurance coverage often makes prescription drugs cheaper than over-the-counter drugs, which in turn makes for very crowded waiting rooms. It's cheaper to see the doctor than to buy cold medicine at the drug store, so everyone goes to the hospital for the smallest of aches and pains.

The crowds in the waiting rooms and the speed with which a doctor often is forced to see a patient leaves many foreigners with the impression that the Japanese medical system is cold and uncaring. Still, Japan's medical standards are high and the quality of treatment is quite good.

People not covered by employees' insurance can join the National Health Insurance Plan *(Kokumin Kenkou Hoken)*. The monthly premiums for the plan are calculated by multiplying your resident's tax for the previous year by 107 percent, adding a flat fee, then dividing the sum by 12. Since resident's tax is based on your previous year's income, you pay no resident's tax and only a fixed monthly fee for national insurance during your first year in Japan.

You can join the National Health Insurance Plan at your city or ward office. Once you join the plan you cannot quit until you leave Japan or join another health plan. Part of your premium is refunded when you leave the plan, so don't forget to let the city or ward people know if you leave.

14

Under the National Health Insurance Plan the government pays approximately 70 percent of the costs for medical and dental treatment. Employees' health insurance can cover as much as 90 percent of most medical and dental care costs.

Cosmetic surgery, general physical examinations, immunizations, normal childbirth and purposely inflicted injuries or injuries resulting from an attempted suicide are not covered by health insurance.

When you join the National Health Insurance Plan or any other insurance plan you get a card or booklet to verify your membership. When you visit a doctor, dentist or hospital for the first time they will ask for the booklet or card. After your first visit most hospitals issue their own cards, which you must show whenever you visit the hospital again. Some cards are like business cards, while others resemble credit cards. In general, a card for one hospital or clinic is not valid at any other.

Your insurance is good at any institution that accepts it. Many clinics and hospitals that cater to foreigners do not accept National Health Insurance, and some don't take any insurance, so check before you go.

Your choice for medical care is between the medical practitioner and the general hospital. The two are often compared to individually-run shops and large department stores to better illustrate their differences. General hospitals are large, have the newest equipment and are conveniently near stations, but they're also crowded and you can spend a lot of time in the waiting room. The medical practitioner works on a smaller scale, but the waiting time is shorter and the care seems more personal.

Going to a Japanese Hospital

The first place to go is the reception desk. If it's your first visit, present your insurance card or booklet, or if you've used the hospital before and have a hospital card, present that at the reception desk. If you don't have insurance, explain to the receptionist. Describe your illness or ask specifically for the department you want to visit.

In larger hospitals you will be sent to the reception window of the department you need, then to a waiting area. In smaller hospitals you'll be sent straight to a waiting room. There you'll wait until your turn comes and your name is called.

You can make most consultations smoother by being able to answer the following questions:

    1) How long have you had your illness?

    2) What are the specifics of your illness?

    3) Have you had this illness before?

Have your medical history ready as well, such as:

    1) Are you taking any medication now?

    2) What kind of diseases or illnesses have you had in the past?

    3) What diseases are common in your family? (Diabetes, hypertension, heart disease, etc.)

    4) Do you have any allergies? Is there any medication you cannot take?

After your consultation, the receptionist will call you and give you your bill and any medicines prescribed. Be sure to take some cash with you, as hospitals don't take credit cards. Most hospitals have their own pharmacies and fill their own prescriptions.

Japanese hospitals are relatively autonomous, and a hospital can only be used by the doctors employed there. If an ambulance takes you to a hospital other than the one you normally use, your doctor from the other hospital cannot treat you. Patient transfers between hospitals are very rare.

What Hospitals are Open on Sundays and Holidays?

Most hospitals and clinics in Japan close or offer only limited service on Sundays and holidays. Area hospitals and clinics agree ahead of time which facilities will stay open during which holidays, and the schedule is on a rotating basis. To find which services near you are open, check at your city or ward office, or at your local public health center.

Dental Care

Japan's dentists are also divided into those that work in general hospitals and those that practice privately. The private practitioners are more convenient for check-ups, fillings and cleanings, but the general hospitals are better for specialized work. Most routine dental work is covered by your health insurance, but some procedures and treatments are not.

Dental work on Sundays and holidays is available on the same rotating basis as medical treatment at those times.

The Public Health Center

Your public health center is there to make sure public health and sanitation standards are met. They offer examinations for tuberculosis, geriatric diseases and other general health problems, and counseling for pregnancy and childbirth, child-raising and other issues. They offer many free or inexpensive services. Check with your local center for more details.

Where Can I Take an AIDS Test? A VD Test?

Some private hospitals administer tests for AIDS and venereal diseases, but your local public health centers may be cheaper and more convenient.

If you don't speak Japanese, it's best to have someone who does call your health center for details as to the cost and procedures. Most health centers administer tests a few times a month on specific days, but the days vary with the health center. A reservation is required in most cases.

You don't have to give your name, and they won't ask to see your ARC or any identification, so you can remain anonymous.

Don't expect to find anyone who speaks English at the health center, and if you don't speak Japanese, go with someone who does.

Health centers offer the least expensive tests in the Tokyo area. An AIDS test at a Tokyo health center costs about ¥1,600.

The health center will give you the date your results are expected back, usually about two weeks from the testing date. Return to the health center on the specified day to pick up your results.

Health centers cannot provide treatment, so go to a local hospital if your test turns out positive. Bigger hospitals are more likely than small clinics to offer treatment for venereal diseases.

The health centers handle AIDS and VD questions and consultations, or you can call the Tokyo Metropolitan Health Department at 03-5320-4485.

Additionally, the Japan HIV Center operates an AIDS information and counseling hotline in English. The service is available Saturdays from 1:00pm to 6:00pm. In-person advice and counseling is also available. Call for more information.

Japan HIV Center English Hotline   03-5256-3002

What Should I Do If I Leave Something in the Train/Taxi/Bus?

If you leave something in a train, bus or taxi - or most anywhere else in Japan - you have a good chance of getting it back. Briefcases, wallets, purses, cameras and the like all seem to find their ways to lost and found departments, so if you lose something, check the lost and found.

On the Train/Subway

If you leave an item on the train, tell a station attendant as soon as you can. If you've already returned home, call the train/subway line's general information office or their lost and found center. The information office is more likely to have English-speaking staff who can handle your problem, but lost and founds usually have had experience with foreigners losing things.

JR East Infoline	03-3423-0111
JR Tokyo Lost And Found Center	03-3231-1880
JR Shinjuku Lost And Found Center	03-3354-4019
JR Ueno Lost And Found Center	03-3841-8069
Eidan (TRTA) Subway Lost And Found Center	03-3834-5577
Subway Information	03-3837-7111
Toei Lost And Found Center	03-3815-7229

(for Toei subways, buses and the Toden streetcars)

In a Taxi

If you leave an item in a taxi, call the cab company immediately and give them a description of the item and the taxi number from your receipt. If you didn't keep your receipt, and if you don't remember the name of the cab company, call the Kindaika Center. They're not a lost and found, but they can re-connect you with lost goodies.

Tokyo Taxi Kindaika Center (24 hours)   03-3648-0300

The sooner you check with the lost and found, the better your chances of finding your property. Every company has a different system, but most transportation companies forward lost items to the police soon after they're received. If an item has been forwarded, the company involved can tell you which police station to check.

Local police stations keep lost items for one month, then forward them to the Tokyo Metropolitan Police Department's lost and found section.

Tokyo Metro Police Dept. Lost And Found   03-3814-4151

In most cases, *teiki-ken* (commuter passes) that have been found are kept at the station where they were discovered, or forwarded to one of the ends of the pass. The owner's name and sometimes the destinations of the pass will be written on a chalkboard or otherwise posted at that station. In either case, ask a station attendant. It is unlikely that someone else will use your pass.

The only items unlikely to be returned if left unattended are umbrellas when the weather is bad, and cash. If you lose an item in a park or some other public area, check the spot where you think you left the item first, then ask at the local police box.

My Bicycle Disappeared. How Can I Get It Back?

Bicycle traffic is another headache for Tokyo's local authorities, because the great number of bikes parked and piled atop one another can make sidewalks very difficult to pass through.

Some wards and cities impound bikes left in illegal or unauthorized spots. If you park your bike on the sidewalk and it's not there when you go back for it, check with your city or ward office to see where impounded bikes are kept. You usually have to go to the impound lot yourself to reclaim your bike, and there's often a fine or storage charge (in most cases less than ¥2,000).

Authorities in some areas sell or raffle away impounded bikes that go unclaimed for a certain time, and this can be a low-cost way to pick up a bike. Check with your city or ward office, or with the impound officials.

Most areas with heavy bicycle traffic have special bicycle parking lots nearby. Some of these lots only rent spaces on a monthly basis, but others will rent you a spot for the day. Check with a lot attendant to make sure. A fee of ¥100 or so is a fair daily fee.

Register your bicycle with the police or at a local bicycle shop. If it is stolen and the police recover it, they will return it to you.

What Should I Do If I Lose My Passport?

The first thing you should do if you lose your passport is contact your embassy or consulate. They'll tell you all the exact procedures from there, but the general pattern is for you to file a lost-item report *(ishitsu todoke)* with the police. They'll issue a *keisatsu shoumei*, which proves that you have filed a missing item report with them. Most countries require a *keisatsu shoumei*.

Go to the legation with the form, some identification, passport photos (two or three - check with the embassy), and any other documents they request. They'll give you an application for a replacement passport.

The whole process takes about three weeks, and the replacement charges and handling fees will cost ¥5,000 to ¥10,000.

Sometimes lost passports will be forwarded to the embassy, so there's a chance it'll turn up there.

Telephone numbers of selected embassies are in the appendix.

After contacting your embassy, call the Tokyo Metropolitan Police Department's lost and found section (see p. 21) or Police Information (see p. 10).

How Do I Get an Alien Registration Certificate (ARC)?

If you are a foreign national in Japan, you are required to register with your city or ward office within 90 days of your arrival unless:

1) You have been granted permission for provisional landing, port of call landing, in-transit landing, landing as a crew member, emergency landing or landing due to disaster.

2) You hold 4-1-1 (diplomat) or 4-1-2 (government official) resident status.

3) You are a member or civilian employee of the U.S. armed forces or United Nations forces, or a dependent of the same.

4) You will leave Japan within 90 days of your arrival. Otherwise, you need to go to the Registration Section (*Koseki-gakari*) of the Citizens' Affairs Department (*Shimin-ka*) at your city or ward office and register.

To register you need:

   a) An application for alien registration (available at the city or ward office and with the vital parts in English)
   b) Your passport
   c) Two 5×5cm photos of the upper half of your torso, without a hat. The photos must be made from the same negative and must have been taken within the past six months.

d) Your left index finger. The law requiring a print of this finger <u>has</u> been revised, but the revision is not yet in effect (as of October, 1992). Until it is, your fingerprint will be enshrined in public records.

They'll give you a form saying that you have applied for registration and indicating when you can pick up the Alien Registration Certificate *(Gaikokujin Touroku Shoumeisho)* itself. It's usually a two week wait, after which you'll have about a week to pick it up.

The ARC is pretty important. You are required to keep it with you at all times and to show it to immigration officials or police on demand. If you don't have your ARC with you, and if you don't have your passport either, you have no way to prove you are in Japan legally. You probably will be hauled off to the station until somebody brings one or the other to you (you won't be allowed to get it yourself). Your ARC is very much like your umbrella, in that you never need it when you have it, but the one time you're without it....

Alien Registration Certificates issued today are small laminated cards that resemble Japanese driver's licenses. An earlier version of the certificate came in booklet form, which made it a real nuisance to carry around in a wallet or purse.

Changes in Your ARC

Whenever any of the information listed on the ARC changes (your address, your visa status, etc.), you must report these changes to your city or ward office within 14 days. Bring anything that might be required to verify the changes.

If Your ARC is Lost or Stolen

If your ARC is lost or stolen you must apply for a new one at your city or ward office within 14 days of the loss, but it's safer to apply for reissue as soon as possible. You need to take your passport and two photos with you.

Certificate of Having an Alien Registration Certificate

Having your ARC, with your photo and fingerprint on the front, is not proof that you actually have your ARC. At odd times you will be asked for official reasons to come up with the *Gaikokujin Touroku Zumi-Shoumeisho*, which is a certificate proving you have an Alien Registration Certificate. It sounds stupid, but the second certificate is required from time to time. Your city or ward office will sell you one for about ¥200.

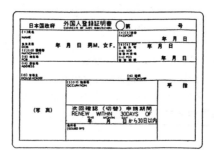

2 Help in Daily Living

How Do I Divide Burnable and Non-Burnable Trash?

Japanese divide their garbage into that which is burnable and that which is non-burnable. The burnable is burned and the non-burnable disposed of in other ways, but what exactly is burnable and what is not causes no end of debate.

The Tokyo Metropolitan Sanitation Department's General Affairs Section puts the following types of garbage in the non-burnable heading:

1) Glass, metal objects, sharp objects and items that could cause injury.

2) Plastics, including plastic bags, dental floss, plastic plates and utensils, trays, plastic wrap, and plastic bottles.

3) Leather goods, like briefcases, handbags, shoes, and belts.

4) Rubber goods, such as sandals, balls and rubber hoses.

Burnable garbage consists mainly of papers and paper items, food garbage, playing cards, milk and juice cartons, cloth and clothes, catalogs and newspapers.

Despite the contradiction, it's okay to put your non-burnable garbage out in plastic bags. In most parts of Tokyo burnable garbage is collected three times a week and non-burnable garbage once. Which type of garbage is picked up on what day varies with your neighborhood, so ask your neighbors for specifics.

If you put your non-burnables out on the burnable day, or if you put your bag of non-burnables in the collection spot for the burnables, you'll irritate both the garbage people and your neighbors. Also, if you put it out before collection day the dogs and cats - or the huge crows that haunt Tokyo - might spread your garbage up and down the street. Your neighbors will not appreciate this, either.

Having been divided into the above categories, some garbage can be disposed of in other ways. In the past, some neighborhoods would trade rolls of toilet paper for your old newspapers, but the price of newspaper dropped and in most cases the service has been discontinued. Nevertheless, most areas still have some system of newspaper collection, usually twice a month.

Despite the inclusion of glass and metal objects in the non-burnable group, most areas have specific days for the collection of cans and bottles. Again, check with your neighbors or your city or ward office for specifics. Can and bottle day usually comes twice a month. The day before can and bottle day someone in the neighborhood will put plastic bins on the street. One bin is for cans, one is for bottles.

Broken glass goes with non-burnables, not cans and bottles. When you put broken glass out, keep it in a box or open bag, so garbage collectors can see it's dangerous and handle it gently.

Milk and juice cartons, though in the burnable group, can be dropped off for recycling at some supermarkets. Check your area for stores that offer this service.

Some neighborhoods have collection bins for used batteries, and some electrical appliance stores (or other places where batteries are sold) also accept batteries.

Do not pour used cooking oil down the drain. Instead, wait for it to cool, then add *gyouko-zai*, a solidifying agent. Let the oil harden, then throw it away with the burnables.

Non-burnable garbage

Burnable garbage

Where are the solidifying agents for cooking oil?—
—*Gyouko-zai wa doko desu ka?*

Garbage	*Gomi*
Burnable garbage	*Moeru gomi* (or) *kanenbutsu*
	燃えるゴミ　　可燃物
Non-burnable garbage	*Moenai gomi* (or) *funenbutsu*
	燃えないゴミ　　不燃物
Can	*Kan*
Bottle	*Bin*

When can I put out my burnable garbage (non-burnable garbage/cans and bottles)?
—*Moeru gomi (moenai gomi/kan to bin) o itsu daseba ii desu ka?*

What is the "Proper" Way to Use a Japanese Toilet? A Japanese Bath?

The Japanese Toilet

It's nothing to be embarrassed about. It's an essential part of life. Many Western toilets here have instructions on them in Japanese - complete with illustrations - so it's no shame to admit a little unfamiliarity with Japan's model.

Some people swear by the Japanese toilet, while others go to great lengths to avoid it. However, it is difficult to avoid a one-on-one with the Japanese version altogether. Many major department stores, train stations and office buildings have Western toilets or both types, but the deeper into rural Japan you go the more the Japanese model dominates. Life will be a little more convenient once you learn the basics of the Japanese toilet.

Basic of basics, check for toilet paper. It is not always a standard item in public toilets, especially in train stations. If toilet paper is not furnished, you can usually find a vending machine for it in the area.

The front of the Japanese toilet is the part with the raised bowl. Position yourself facing the bowl and over the pit. When you squat, make sure your pants are below your knees. If not, loose change, keys, wallets, passports and the like can tumble into the the pit.

Westerners are not the only ones to complain that the Japanese toilet can be rough on the knees, and bars have been added in front or to the right of some toilets, so you can pull yourself up.

If you use the facilities in a home, you will often find a pair of slippers just inside the bathroom door. These are the "bathroom slippers". Put these on and leave your "indoor slippers" outside the bathroom. Switch back when you leave. Do not wear "bathroom slippers" outside the bathroom.

The Bath

When using a bath in a private home (*ofuro*) or a public bath (*sentou*), the thing to remember is that the tub is for soaking your body, not cleaning it. Wash yourself thoroughly and rinse off all traces of soap <u>before</u> you enter the tub. You will upset a lot of people if you bring the soap into the tub with you at a *sentou*. The attendants will close the place while they clean and rinse the tub. If you do this at a private home, you might upset your hosts, whether or not they reveal their irritation to you.

Another no-no is pulling the plug. When Japanese leave the tub after a long soak, they leave the water in for the next person to use. Draining the tub when you finish seems rude and selfish, so leave the water in when you're done, and replace the boards or the mat that goes over the top to keep the water hot.

Japanese tubs are typically very, very hot, so test the water temperature before you get in. If it's too hot for you, you don't have to get in. If you do get in, it won't seem as hot if you keep perfectly still.

How Should I Go About Finding a Place to Live?

In the ideal scenario, you're in Tokyo as an employee of some large corporation that found a large house for you, is underwriting all your living expenses, paying you a huge cost-of-living adjustment and other nice things like that.

When you came to Tokyo in the second best scenario, your company had found an apartment for you already, so all you had to do was unpack your bags.

In the most common case you're here, you need a place to live, and you're not sure where to start.

Long-Term Housing

If you plan to stay in Japan for a while, you'll probably need an apartment. However, before you start looking for a place you should write out exactly what kind of place you have in mind. Where do you want to live? How much time do you want to spend commuting between work and home? How much do you want to pay? Do you want a Japanese-style apartment or not? How big (small?) an apartment do you want? For your first step, rank these considerations and others in order from "can't live without" to "doesn't matter".

There are three main ways to find a place to live in Japan, and smart apartment hunters use them all. No matter how you find your apartment, you'll probably have to make the final transaction through a real estate agent.

The first way to find an apartment is to check the

English-language publications for ads and information about what's on the market. Most apartments advertised in newspapers are very, very expensive, and once you shock yourself into the expensive reality of Tokyo housing you'll appreciate "normal" Tokyo prices a bit more readily.

The monthly Tokyo Journal usually has a number of ads for more reasonably priced housing in its classified section, and many of the realtors that advertise there have experience dealing with foreigners. CitySource and the English Yellow Pages have long lists of real estate agents ready to work with you.

There are a number of Japanese-language publications to help with the housing search, such as *Shuukan Ruumugaido, Shuukan Juutaku Jouhou* and *Shuukan Apaato Manshon Jouhou (Apaman)*. They add a Japanese point of view to your search, and open a wider range of possibilities. Even so, ads in Japanese aim primarily at Japanese clients, and not every realtor is willing or able to handle a foreign client.

The second way to find an apartment is to go directly to a realtor. You can call one and ask what's available, or if you have an idea of the area you want to live in, wander around the vicinity and look at the ads realtors post on bulletin boards outside their offices (see below). If you don't speak Japanese, ask a friend who does to go along with you. Be prepared to tell the realtor your price range, the size you want and other details.

The third way to find an apartment is to ask around. The more people that know you're looking for an apartment, the more people that can help you out or share their information with you. Bulletin boards at school or work can have useful information, so check around and ask your friends and co-workers to do the same.

When you've found an apartment you like, talk to the realtor. Brace yourself, because you can find some very unpleasant things in the realtor's office.

Ugliness Number One: Japanese laws do not prohibit landlords from descriminating against people on the basis of their race or nationality. Many landlords don't want to deal with the real or imagined language and cultural differences that come with a foreign tenant, and they flatly refuse to deal with foreigners.

If that's not a problem, and you've found a place you like, you can prevent other people from renting it by paying *tetsukekin*. When you pay *tetsukekin*, you commit yourself to eventually renting the apartment, though the contract details will be worked out in the future. When you sign the contract, the money you paid for *tetsukekin* is credited to your *reikin* (see below). If you change your mind and don't rent the place, your money is not returned. *Tetsukekin* is normally one month's rent.

As a foreigner, you probably need a Japanese to be your *hoshounin*, or guarantor. The guarantor agrees that he'll take full responsibility if you break your lease. Your company will probably act as your guarantor if necessary.

With the signing of the contract, you probably need to pay a deposit, or *shikikin*. *Shikikin* is typically two months' rent. It is returned to you when you move out after damages, if any, have been subtracted.

After *shikikin* comes Ugliness Number Two, *reikin*. This is key money, often described as "thank you" money to your landlord for services to be rendered. It's a non-refundable gift to your landlord that you have to pay or, in most cases, you won't get the apartment. Though not all landlords require key money, some want it every time the contract is renewed. In most other major countries, *reikin* is somewhere between extortion and bribery and is very illegal. In Japan, *reikin* is about two months' rent.

On top of the variable *shikikin* and *reikin*, the realtors also get their due. The real estate agent's fee is typically one month's rent.

With *shikikin*, *reikin*, realty fees and first month's rent, you can expect to pay six month's rent before you even get a key. For a small apartment at ¥80,000 a month, that's ¥480,000!

Reading the Realtor's Ads

An advertisement on a real estate agent's bulletin board or window will look something like this:

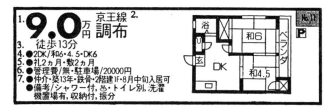

1. The 9.0 shows that the rent for this apartment is ¥90,000 a month.
2. The closest station and the line
3. The time it takes to the station on foot
4. The number of rooms in the apartment (see below), their styles and their sizes
5. The number of month's rent for *reikin* and *shikikin*
6. The monthly maintenance fee, if any, and the monthly fee if you want a space in the building's parking lot
7. The age of the building and its construction

The typical description of an apartment begins with the number and size of its rooms. A kitchen with a little bit of space in which to eat is referred to as a DK, for dining kitchen. A kitchen with more space than a DK is an LDK, for living room, dining room, kitchen. Other rooms are usually assigned numbers, so an apartment with two rooms and a kitchen with a bit of extra space is a 2DK, a large kitchen and three other rooms is a 3LDK and so on.

The sizes of the kitchen, DK or LDK are not often in the ad, but measurements of the other rooms are. The style of the room (Western or Japanese) is indicated by a character. Japanese style means the room has a tatami mat floor and is measured by the number of mats. Western style means the floor is not tatami, but no other details are usually given. Western style rooms are measured in square meters or by the number of mats it would have if it were Japanese style. One mat is roughly 90×180cm.

If the toilet and bath are in separate rooms, the toilet symbol is used for the toilet and a character for the bath. The letters UB, for unit bath, indicate the toilet and bath are in the same room.

Short-Term Housing

If you're not sure how long you'll be staying in Tokyo, or if you can't afford to move into an apartment yet, short-term housing is available. The most common option for foreigners are dormitory-like "gaijin houses".

Some gaijin houses charge deposits, but few demand key money. They are available on a monthly, weekly, or in some cases daily basis. Most gaijin houses offer single and shared rooms.

As the name implies, most people living in gaijin houses are foreigners. This can give you many insights into other cultures and many different perspectives from which to view Japan. Networking with your neighbors can provide employment leads, information on cheap places to shop and other benefits.

On the down side, toilets and showers in many gaijin houses are public, which can cause a lot of trouble when everyone wants to use the facilities at the same time. The atmosphere of a gaijin house depends on the people living there. If everyone respects everyone else's rights to quiet, privacy, etc., a gaijin house can be a good place to live. If residents go out of their way to antagonize each other, it can be a living hell.

Tokyo Journal carries ads for a number of gaijin houses in its classified section, and other foreigners can recommend one to you or find someone who can. Visit a couple before you decide on one, just to get an idea of what's available. As always, shop around.

How Can I Get Rid of Insects?

Central Tokyo is relatively free from mosquitos because it doesn't have many ponds, parks or other suitable places for eggs to hatch.

The suburbs, however, with apartment buildings and shopping centers interspersed with fields and empty lots, are not so lucky and the stretch of hot weather from the rainy season through September is mosquito season.

One of most effective mosquito countermeasures is the *katori-senkou*, or incense coil. They are sold in drug stores and supermarkets for about ¥200 a box, or about ¥800 for a big can of coils. Light the end of a coil and place it on a plate or some other heat-resistant tray (some *katori-senkou* sets come with their own trays). Don't put a coil on the floor or anywhere it could start a fire.

The incense from the coil weakens mosquitos, making them less likely to bother people and easier to kill. The smell can be pretty strong, so keep the plate near an open window or some other flow of air.

Electric versions of *katori-senkou* are also available at drug stores and the like. A product called Vape (*beepu* in katakana) for example, does a similar job by dispersing small amounts of a insecticide into the air at regular intervals. One bottle of liquid insecticide can last up to 30 days.

Additionally, mosquito repellants and other sprays are

available at drug stores, department stores and many convenience stores.

Where are the incense coils?—
> *— Katori-senkou wa doko desu ka?*

Where is the mosquito repellant?—
> *— Mushi-yoke supureei wa doko desu ka?*

Dani

Dani are little ticks that live and breed in your tatami and carpets, your curtains, and other places in your car, apartment and office. In addition to burrowing into your skin and itching like the devil, they are thought to play some part in a number of allergies. They are most active in July and August when humidity is high, but they can attatch themselves to you at almost any time. You'll never kill all the *dani* in your home, but you can reduce their numbers if you take steps before they hatch.

Dani like warmth, but hate heat, so if you have *them* in your carpet, hang it over your balcony on a sunny day. Turn it over after a while, so that both sides get some exposure to the sun. The heat will weaken or kill a lot of *dani*, and you can get rid of the bodies and eggs if you beat the carpet with a futon beater or the like. The same process works on the *dani* in your futon, which is why on any sunny day the air is alive with the bwup-bwup-bwup of people beating their bedding.

Your vacuum cleaner is the best weapon against *dani* in items you can't hang over your balcony. Some machines have special anti-*dani* settings designed to suck up the little monsters, but that's not necessary. The main point is to go over an area several times - not just once.

There are cleaning services to rid your futon of *dani*. If you think you need this service, ask your local dry cleaners if they can do it. The cost is around ¥3,000-¥3,500 per futon.

The vacuum cleaner is also effective against *dani* in your chairs, sofas, and the seats of your car. Use a small nozzle for more suction, and sweep an area several times before moving on to the next.

Dani like curtains, also. If your curtains aren't washable, vacuum them as you did your carpet, covering a small area thoroughly before moving on to the next. Be sure and vacuum your curtain rails as well.

One of the nastiest things about *dani* is that they are shameless enough to infest even your stuffed animals. If your washable teddy bear becomes a playground for *dani*, wash him with a kitchen detergent, then wrap him in a towel and dry him with a hair dryer. Leave teddy out overnight to air out. If teddy is not washable, you can still kill a lot of his *dani* if you put him in a plastic bag and leave him outside on a hot day. Vacuum him afterwards, to remove any *dani* remains.

There is a "*dani* hotline" for more anti-*dani* strategies and information on the connection between *dani* and allergies. It is, however, only in Japanese, so ask a friend for help.

Dani Hotline (Monday through Friday 2:00pm-4:00pm)
03-3451-2463

Cockroaches

"Roach motel" style traps are one of the most common ways of getting rid of your cockroaches. There are a number of different types of traps available at your local drug store or supermarket, the most memorable of which are shaped and colored like little houses.

There are also a number of sprays and poisons on the market, most of which require no special instructions.

Cute traps aside, the best way to keep roaches away is to keep your home clean and dry. For instance, can and bottle day only comes twice a month, so rinse out your empties before you bag them. Do the same to your food-related non-burnable garbage like styrofoam meat trays. Keep your food garbage sealed tightly in a plastic bag and take care to clean up after meals.

What Can I Do to Get Rid of This MOLD???

Japan is a country with a <u>lot</u> of rain. First, there's the rainy season, then an incredibly hot and humid summer, then the typhoon season... it never seems to stop. All the wetness and warmth makes an ideal playground for mold and mildew. If you're not careful, you can find it in your closet, under your sink, in the bathroom... anywhere.

Beating Mold

Weapons for your war against mold are waiting for you at your local supermarkets and department stores. Ask the staff "*Kabi-tori-zai wa doko desu ka?*" ("Where are the mold and mildew killers?"), and they'll point you in the right direction.

Kabi is Japanese for "mold and mildew", and many mold-fighting products have *kabi* in their names. Examples are *Kabi-kiraa* (Kabi Killer), *Kabi-tori* (Kabi Remover), and *Kabi no Gaado* (Kabi Guard).

Bath and Toilet Mold

Because your toilet and bath are usually dark, warm and damp, they're the easiest places for mold to grow. But there are some products that will help keep mold in check, if not kill it altogether. *Bou-kabi Meji Ichiban,* for example, is a set of two pens. One pen kills the mold between the tiles in your bathroom, the other fills the space with a white mold-resistant paint.

In your shower you may find a <u>mop</u> more helpful. It can cover more territory than a hand rag, and it's easy to use on ceilings and other hard-to-reach places. Dip it in your mold-killer of choice and use it like a normal mop, but be sure to wear protective eye and hand gear. Most mold killers are rough on your skin and potentially poisonous, so open your doors and windows and keep fresh air circulating.

Closet and Wardrobe Mold

It's easier to beat *kabi* in your closet and wardrobe by stopping it from springing up in the first place. For this, you want desiccants or dehydrators, or *kan-sou-zai*. These absorb a lot of the moisture from the back corners of your closet and wardrobe. Like *kabi-tori-zai*, you can find dehydrators by asking at your store "*kan-sou-zai wa doko desu ka?*"

Kan-sou-zai are often sold in sets of three, and triangular shapes are popular because they fit better in the corners of your closet. Two units will keep a normal sized closet dry for a good while, and one will do the same for a wardrobe.

To use *kan-sou-zai*, remove the plastic wrapper and plastic lid from a unit, then tear off the foil lid. Do not tear off the paper under the foil sheet. Replace the plastic lid, then place the unit in a corner of your closet.

Check the unit from time to time, and replace it when it fills with water. It won't absorb any more moisture when the desiccating agent is all used up.

Tatami Mold

If you're away from your home for any length of time, particularly during the summer or the rainy season, don't be too surprised to find mold and mildew waiting to welcome you home. Mold and mildew are not limited to your bathroom or closet. In the worst cases, they can come right out onto your tatami mats and turn your whole floor green or black. But like *kabi* in other places, if you start early enough, you can remove tatami mold easily.

To clean *kabi* from your tatami, rub the affected area briskly with a rag that has been dipped in mold-killer.

Don't rub the tatami against the grain, and don't drench the floor with the *kabi-tori-zai*, as both are bad for tatami.

After you remove most of the mess and let the tatami air out, go over the tatami again with a different rag and with disinfectant or rubbing alcohol in place of mold-killer.

Other Mold

Kabi can crop up in your refrigerator as well, and for this mold a potentially poisonous mold-remover is <u>not</u> what you need. You can safely remove mold from the insulating linings of your fridge with rubbing alcohol.

General steps to prevent outbreaks of mold and mildew include airing out and drying out closets, bathrooms and other places mold is likely to appear. Smaller items susceptible to mold, like drawers and bath items, can be exposed to sunlight and fresh air to stop mold's return.

Mold knows no mercy. Like the *dani* that shamelessly nest in your stuffed animals, mold will crop up on clothes in the back of your closet, your shoes, your baseball glove and, yes, your stuffed animals too.

Is There Any Special Etiquette for Visiting a Japanese Friend?

Japanese don't have a strong tradition of inviting people into their homes. The home is a private place, and besides, it's pretty small. If a friend never invites you to his home, it's not a sign that there's some secret animosity or ill will, it's just a reflection of Japanese culture.

If your friend <u>does</u> invite you home there are no set rules of etiquette to follow. When Japanese visit other people they usually bring along a small gift, but this is more a nice gesture than a social rule. If you want to take a gift, think of what your friend would like to get. If you can't come up with any ideas, flowers or wine are reliable and easy to find standbys. If you visit often, you don't have to take a gift every time, and if you are close friends you probably don't need to take a gift at all.

An expression Japanese often use when they enter someone else's house is "*ojama shimasu*". The literal meaning is along the lines of "I'm going to be rude", or "I'm going to be troublesome", but its widely accepted as an apology for imposing on someone. Give your present to your host after you're met at the door. If your present is wrapped, your host might not open it right away. If not, don't feel insulted, and don't push your host to open it.

In most things it is safe to follow your host's lead, but if you've been invited over for dinner, your hosts might wait for you to begin eating before they do. Just before Japanese eat they say "*itadakimasu*", which means "I accept (this food)". After the meal they say "*gochisou sama deshita*", which is roughly "it was a feast".

When you leave, "*ojama shimashita*", "I have troubled you", is a good parting phrase.

Dropping by uninvited is usually frowned upon in Japan. Even with close friends, it's a good idea to call before you visit.

Phrases and Uses

Gomen kudasai	Excuse me (used to get someone's attention when knocking at a door)
Ojama shimasu	I'm going to bother you (used when first shown into a house or apartment)
Ojama shimashita	I've troubled you (past tense of "*Ojama shimasu*". Use it when leaving your host's home)
Itadakimasu	I accept (this food) (Say this before you start eating)
Gochisou sama deshita	It was a feast (Say this after your meal)

When Do Japanese Give Gifts, and What Do They Give?

Japanese seem to enjoy giving gifts, and Japan has many occasions for Japanese and non-Japanese alike to give and receive gifts.

The first regular gift-giving event of the year is *Otoshidama*, in the first days of each new year. Adults give the children around them money or other presents.

If you are going to turn twenty in the coming year, you can celebrate Coming of Age Day (*Seijin no Hi*, January 15). New adults get all sorts of adult-type gifts from their families. Typical gifts are business clothes and money for travel.

Valentine's Day in Japan is for women to give candy and presents to men. Men are expected to return the favor on White Day, March 14.

Late March and early April bring graduations and the job hunting season. Only family members give the graduate gifts, which often include business-wear and work-related items. The trains fill with sharply yet conservatively dressed young people with briefcases and resumes in hand.

Successful acceptance into a school or university is another gift-giving occasion for the student's close family. Cash, usually ¥3,000 to ¥7,000, is the most common gift.

Mother's Day and Father's Day are observed, and the gifts of choice are as in the West, carnations for Mom and marginally useful items for Dad.

The first part of July marks the summer gift-giving season, *Ochuugen*. Japanese send thank-you gifts to people who've helped them out in the past year or so. The gift and value are the sender's choice, and there are a number of items to choose from. Boxed sets of peanuts, melons, instant coffee and beer are all popular choices. Companies also send gifts to valued customers.

November 15 is *Shichi-go-san*, when three, five and seven year-olds put on their formal clothes and celebrate their coming of age with a visit to the local shrine. Like *Otoshidama, Shichi-go-san* is another chance for kids to get a little cash from their relatives.

In mid-December comes *Oseibo*, which is a second *Ochuugen*, a gift to anyone who's been helpful in the recent past. Coincidentally, *Ochuugen* and *Oseibo* arrive at about the time most Japanese get their bonuses. Japanese bonuses can be the equivilent of around three months' pay, but even when a worker gets a hefty bonus he still has to spend a lot of it on thank-you gifts.

Christmas in Japan is more a romantic event than a religious one. Spending the night with a lover in a hotel that overlooks Tokyo Bay is the ideal Christmas Eve for many young Japanese. On the more sentimental side, gifts are exchanged between family members and close friends.

The standard Japanese wedding gift is cash, and the amount varies with the giver's relationship to the couple. The average for friends is about ¥20,000 per person, and protocol calls for crisp new bills in a *shuugi-bukuro* (a special envelope sold in stationery and convenience stores).

Cash is also the expected condolence gift for a funeral, and there is another special envelope, a *bushuugi-bukuro*.

From ¥6,000 to ¥10,000 is typical, and new bills are not necessary.

The only difference in funeral and wedding attire for men is the color of the necktie. Black or dark suits and white shirts are the standard, with white neckties for weddings and black ones for funerals. Wedding attire for women has no set requirements, only that it look formal. Black or dark dresses are the norm for funerals.

What Do I Need to Marry a Japanese?

Before a foreigner can marry a Japanese national in Japan both parties must meet the requirements of their home countries. These requirements vary from country to country, so check with your embassy or consulate. If you meet the conditions, they will issue a certificate or affidavit stating such, which will be in the native language. A Japanese translation of the certificate is required, and if the legation does not provide you with one, you must get one on your own.

Take the affidavit and translation, your passport, and a form called the *Konin Todoke*, to the Family Registration Section (*Koseki-gakari*) of your city or ward office. The Japanese national needs only an official copy of his/her family register.

Your city or ward office can give you a *Konin Todoke* form. Pick it up ahead of time. Getting married isn't too difficult, but check with your legation and to make sure everything is in order. If you don't have the right documents at the right times, getting married can be very troublesome.

What's the Best Way to Study Japanese?

Why Study Japanese?

Until you learn the basics of the Japanese language you're doomed to stumble your way around Japan, hoping there'll always be someone to help you out. That's not really as bad as it might seem, because English has been a required subject in Japanese schools since the Meiji Era. But you came to Japan. You're here. You might at least try to learn the language.

There are a lot of options for people wanting to study the Japanese language. A Japanese language school is the most obvious, but there are a number of public and private groups that offer instruction as well. Additionally, you can teach yourself, or you can trade language lessons with a friend. The best method for learning depends on your purposes for learning and the amount of time you plan to devote to your studies. If you want to speak Japanese, why spend time on reading and writing? If you're just going to use Japanese with your friends, why study the formal speech of *keigo*? Do you have the time to study several hours each day, or does your schedule only allow a little time here and there for study? Decide what your goals are, and proceed from there.

The Japanese Language School

Most language schools offer classes at several times

throughout the day, so you can study when you have space in your schedule. You have the most flexibility in scheduling your classes if you are taking private or one-on-one lessons. Many schools can send instructors to your company, and some can send them to your home, but this usually costs extra.

You can get a student visa if you are taking classes full time (20 hours a week), if the language school agrees to sponsor you, and if you meet some other requirements. Talk to the language schools for details.

One point to remember is that people from countries that have languages based on *kanji*, Chinese characters, have a big advantage over you when it comes to reading and writing Japanese. Their conversational skills can be at a beginner's level, but people with a strong knowledge of *kanji* can understand passages written in Japanese fairly well. If you're only studying conversation, this shouldn't matter much, but if you're studying reading and writing, be ready for the challenge.

Another thing to look for in a language class is a low student-teacher ratio. The best classes are one-on-one, or in groups of three or four where students and instructor can interact in the language. A class of 40 people in an auditorium discourages participation, and practice and participation are essential to language learning.

Most schools offer free trial lessons, and it is to your benefit to sit through one to see if it's the kind of lesson you want. If you have a chance, ask students at the school what they think of their classes. Why did they choose their school over all the others? Do they think they're getting their money's worth? What do they think are the school's strengths and weaknesses? Shop around.

To find language schools check CitySource, the classified sections of English-language newspapers and Tokyo Journal, but best of all, ask other foreigners.

City and Ward Services

Many cities and wards provide Japanese instruction as a public service. The classes are usually inexpensive or free, so your only expenses can be the texts and the commute. Still, they don't have the flexibility in scheduling that you can get from a language school. Contact your local city or ward office for more details. In some cases these services are open only to residents of the city or ward.

As an example, Chiyoda Ward has programs that meet twice a week for four months. Classes for beginners and advanced students meet for two hours in the afternoon, and classes for beginners only meet in the evenings. Attendance is limited to people living, working or studying in Chiyoda Ward, and teaching materials are the only expenses (¥3,000).

In addition to publicly funded services, there are a number of volunteer groups that offer Japanese lessons or language exchange. Like city or ward-sponsored classes, lessons from volunteer groups are usually inexpensive or free.

Teaching Yourself

There are a number of sources available to help you teach yourself Japanese. Textbooks, crash course texts, reading guides, tapes and transcripts are all available at bookstores that serve Tokyo's foreign community. NHK airs a Japanese course (a good reason to pay your NHK bill), with texts easily available. The drawback with teaching yourself is that you don't get the interaction you need to communicate your thoughts quickly and effectively. Your reading, writing and comprehension skills may improve significantly, but your speaking skills probably won't.

Trading Lessons

Trading language lessons with a Japanese friend can be an effective way to learn Japanese. The advantages are that the exchanges are less likely to be formal and stiff, and both you and your friend will be more relaxed and unafraid to make mistakes. A drawback is that you may be too relaxed and there will be no pressure or incentive to learn. Its benefits vary with the participants' levels, but language exchange is only as good as its participants are serious.

How Can I Use the Train/ Subway?

The Ticket Machines

One of the machines you'll use the most in Japan is the ticket vending machine. Although the machine itself is one of the easiest to use, language troubles can make deciding which ticket to buy difficult.

Train and subway lines usually place large maps above a station's ticket machines, and fares from that station to all other stations on the map are written near the station names. Put your money in the machine, then push the button for the amount indicated on the fare map. A ticket for that amount and your change, if any, will drop into the tray.

The problem lies with the fare map. How can you find your fare when you can't read your destination on the fare map? Major stations have fare maps in English, but that's only helpful if you're at one of those major stations. If you're at a small station, the odds are against there being an English version of the fare map.

There are at least three ways to overcome this problem.

1) Ask someone. The Japanese people around you know the language. Ask one of them. You can economize words and just ask "Shibuya? Shibuya?" or wherever and hope they figure out what you want, or you can use a complete sentence.

How much to XXXX station?   *XXXX made wa ikura desu ka?*

2) Get a map of your own. Eidan (TRTA) Subway information centers (at most major Eidan stations) have free maps of their lines and information on the use of ticket machines in English. Even if the fare map is in Japanese, compare your English map to the fare map and you can usually figure out the fare for your destination.

3) Buy the cheapest ticket. When you get off, go to the fare adjustment machine or window and pay the remaining fee.

Fare adjustment (window/machine)   *Seisan(jo/ki)*

Fare Adjustment Machines

If your fare is more than the ticket price, when you get off you can pay the difference at a manned ticket gate, at a fare adjustment window, or at a fare adjustment machine. At the gate or window, just give the attendants your ticket and they'll tell you how much you need to pay.

At a fare adjustment machine, insert your ticket or train pass in the slot (usually marked in English), then insert the amount displayed on the screen. Fare adjustment machines only work with tickets that have brown or black backs.

Prepaid Cards

Many train and subway lines offer prepaid cards. JR's Orange Card and the Eidan Metro Card are two examples that are very similar to telephone cards in design and use. Their main advantage is also like that of telephone cards, that you don't need a pocketful of change to ride the train. Most stations on lines that use prepaid cards have at least one ticket vending machine that accepts the cards as well as cash. JR has gone a step further to promote the sale and use of its cards by increasing the number of machines that accept cards only. The advantage to you is that until more people use the cards, lines for card-only machines will be shorter than the cash-only or cash-and-card lines.

Orange Cards sell for ¥1,000, ¥3,000, ¥5,000 and ¥10,000. With the two most expensive ones you get bonuses of ¥300 and ¥700 respectively. As with telephone cards, you can choose from several designs. Most lines that use the cards have card vending machines at every station.

To buy a ticket with a prepaid card, first insert your

card into the machine's card slot. The amount remaining on your card will be shown on the screen. When you select your ticket, the machine will deduct the fare from your card, then give you the ticket and your card. If the amount remaining on your card is less than the fare, you can make up the difference in cash. You cannot, however, make up the difference with another prepaid card.

JR East's iO Card has the same purchasing uses as the Orange Card, but with the iO Card you don't need to buy a ticket. Insert the iO Card directly into an automatic ticket gate just like you would insert a ticket. The gate records the station where you enter the JR East system and the one where you leave, then calculates the appropriate fare and deducts it from the card. The only catch is that you can only use the card with automatic ticket gates and only on the JR lines in the Tokyo area.

All-Day Passes

Many train and subway lines sell have all-day unlimited-use passes. For example, the Eidan lines' one-day all-you-can-ride pass sells for ¥650 and takes you anywhere on the system as many times as you like. Whether you have a planned schedule for your station-hopping, or whether you just want to wander the rails, all-day passes can be pretty convenient.

The Eidan pass sets you free on any line in the Eidan system, but does <u>not</u> permit you to transfer from an Eidan line to a Toei line or other non-Eidan lines. You can buy passes for same-day travel from vending machines at Eidan stations, and for later dates from any Eidan office that sells commuter passes.

The Commuter Pass and Multiple Ticket Packs

If you regularly commute to work or school by train, you should look into buying a commuter pass (*teiki-ken*). You have to fill out a form for your first pass, but after that pass expires you can buy replacement passes from commuter pass machines. If you ride the Keio line to and from Chofu and Shinjuku every weekday for three months you can spend about ¥29,040 for tickets (¥220 one-way), or you can buy a three month *teiki-ken* for ¥22,320.

If you use two different lines to get to work, you can usually have them put on one *teiki-ken*, but if you use three or more lines you'll have to keep track of two separate passes.

Below is a sample application for a three-month *teiki* for Gary Jones between his job near JR Ichigaya Station and his home near JR Nakano Station, going through Shinjuku and Yotsuya along the way. You can use Roman letters if the attendant can understand them, but if there's a mistake you might get a pass for places you don't want to go.

a) Name **b**) Sex **c**) Age (feel free to lie) **d**) The stations you're commuting to and from (in no order) **e**) Transfer points (if any) **f**) The date you want to start using the *teiki* (for first time passes, the day you apply or the following day) **g**) How many months (1, 3, or 6 months) **h**) Your address **i**) Your destination's address **j**) Your phone number **k**) The type of pass (commuting to work or to school)

Kaisuu-ken

If you travel the route regularly, but not everyday, you can save a little money by buying booklets of tickets (*Kaisuu-ken*). Eleven tickets for one way (either way) transit between A and B are sold for the price of ten. They must be used before their expiration date (printed on the booklet). Most lines sell them at ticket offices in major stations along their routes, and some locations have *kaisuu-ken* vending machines. *Kaisuu-ken* are not refundable after you've used the first one of the booklet.

Transfers and Transfer Tickets

Transferring is switching from one train or subway line or system to another. It can be very easy, or it can be time-consuming and frustrating. Transfer tickets are not necessary when switching lines within a system, for example, switching from the Hanzomon line to the Yurakucho line, or from the Toei Shinjuku line to the Toei Mita line. But transferring from one system to another usually means buying another ticket, or buying a transfer ticket.

To buy a transfer ticket for the XXX line, push the button that says "transfer tickets for the XXX line" after you insert your money. Select the fare for your destination you found on the fare map, and collect your ticket. That's all pretty easy.

If you can transfer directly from line A to line B there should be no problem, but any time you have to go through an automatic ticket gate there's a potential for trouble. In certain cases the automatic gate will read your ticket as a ticket with that station as your final destination. In such cases it will keep your ticket, and you'll have to explain to the attendant or buy a new one. To avoid problems like this, go through the manned gate and show the attendant your ticket like you would show him your pass.

If you bought the cheapest ticket and plan to pay the difference when you get off, you usually have to pay wherever you transfer, whether you use the manned or automatic gate.

Smoking Areas

Smokers at any of the Yamanote line's 29 stations can only light up in designated smoking areas. Most lines restrict smokers to certain areas during rush hours, but the Yamanote line keeps their ban in effect all day long.

Commuting Hell

The rush-hour train is one of the many cultural endurance tests you'll face in Japan. It's hard to think of yourself as a cultural ambassador when you're being squeezed, pushed, prodded, stepped on, coughed on and otherwise bounced around your train first thing in the morning. The average Tokyo commute is around an hour, and it's known as *tsuukin jigoku*, or commuting hell. "Hell on wheels" isn't far off, either.

However, the commute is Japan's great equalizer, because everyone is equally likely to be abused, regardless of size, body shape or physical strength. Even when you think you've made it through your ride unscathed, check again. It's not uncommon to find that a fellow inmate in commuting hell has left a pair of lipstick lip-prints on your shirt, blouse or jacket. Explain <u>that</u> away....

How Do I Get Off the Train???

If you've ever been caught in Tokyo's rush hour, you know how circumstances can work against you when it's time to get off the train or subway. At each of the four or five stations since you got on the wall of people has pushed you deeper and deeper into your car. Finally, you've reached your stop, but the train is so packed with people you can't make your way to the doors. In a flash, the wave of people pushing and shoving to get <u>out</u> of the train is replaced by another wave of people pushing and shoving to get <u>into</u> the train- but you still haven't made it to the doors. The incoming wave hits you and pushes you back into the depths of the car, the doors close, and you're off to the next station to try again.

Sure, you could claw and scratch your way out, but that only leads to trouble. You could try "Excuse me", or if you've had a long ride, "Gitouttathaway!" or "Lemmeoutta here!", but wouldn't something in <u>Japanese</u> be more effective? What are the people around you saying when <u>they</u> want to get off?

Two Magic Words
Like "please" and "thank you" in English, Japanese has a few magic words of its own. The next time you're struggling to get off the train, give the magic a try.

1) *Sumimasen*

Sumimasen is a very versitile word. It has several different meanings depending on the situation and context, but in the rush hour trains it usually means something like "excuse me". Slightly less polite variations, like *sum'masen* and *suman*, are also common. Listen to what the people around you are saying and follow their lead.

Sumimasen is also an acceptable apology after you stomp on someone's toes as the train pitches and lurches its way to your destination.

2) *Orimasu*

Orimasu has several homonyms, but when you hear it on the train it means "I'm getting off". Ever so subtle, the speaker is not just keeping you informed of his or her actions ("I'm sitting down," "I'm reading the sports paper," and so on are not announced like "I'm getting off" is), the real meaning is "I'm getting off and you're in my way..." Too subtle? Perhaps. But nicer than "Gitouttathaway".

If you're in a jam, try both. Open with a *sumimasen*, then raise your voice a little and follow with an *orimasu!* Even in the most crowded trains, people usually try to get out of your way if they <u>know</u> you want off.

How Do I Ride a Japanese Bus?

How do I ride a bus in Japan? It seems like an innocent enough question. Is it like buses at home? Where do I pay? How do I let the driver know when I want to get off? How do I know when to get off, for that matter?

Riding a bus is a cheap way to cover short distances, but before you get on one take a good look at a map of its route. Note the stops along the route, because the bus will only stop to pick you up or let you off at designated stops. Make sure the bus stops near your destination.

Board city buses at the front door and put your money in the fare box next to the driver. If you don't have exact change put your coins in a slot near the fare box. If you don't find it right away the driver will point it out to you. The coin slot takes ¥500 and ¥100 coins, and there is also a machine for bills, though most machines will only take ¥1,000 notes. Some machines only break your coins or bills into smaller change, leaving you to put your money in the fare box. Other machines will deduct the fare from the amount you put in, then return you the change, so don't get upset if you put a ¥1,000 note in the machine and don't get ¥1,000 back.

A pre-recorded tape announces the names of the stops as you come to them, and many buses have electric message boards that flash the names of the stops as well. In most cases, however, the names on the tape and the message board are in Japanese, so ask someone for help if you're not sure where your stop is.

When you recognize the name of your stop, or if you know you're near your stop, press one of the stop buttons (often lighted in pink or purple) near you, and exit from the rear door.

Tokyo's buses are ¥180 or ¥200, but different systems are used outside of Tokyo. Buses that cover greater distances often require you to board from the rear door. Take a ticket from the machine to your left as you board. The ticket will have a number corresponding to the place you got on the bus. A fare board at the front of the bus will show the fare from the point you boarded to your present stop, and it increases as you get further from your starting point. When you reach your stop, pay the amount under the number of your ticket and get off by the front door. If you lose your ticket or forget to get one when you board, you may get away with telling the driver where you got on, but you may have to pay the highest charge.

How Do I Take a Taxi in Tokyo?

Catching a taxi in Tokyo is about like catching a taxi anywhere else. Raise your hand and flag one down, wait at a taxi stand, or phone a taxi company. However, Japanese usually don't scream or whistle for cabs.

One problem with the first and most common method is that the taxi you're hailing may already be occupied. The meter in today's Tokyo taxi is linked with the light on the roof, so that when the car is occupied (when the meter is on), the roof light is extinguished. If the top light is on, the cab is vacant. Until July 1, 1992, Tokyo taxis had small, hard to make out green and red "occupied/unoccupied" lights in front of the front passenger's seat. If the light was red, the taxi was potentially yours for the taking. If the light was green, the cab was occupied or off duty. Now Tokyo has fallen in line with most of the rest of the country, but the red/green system is still useful during daylight hours.

If you're waiting at a taxi stand there's no question that eventually you'll get a cab, but the waiting lines at taxi stands can get pretty long, especially just after the trains have stopped running or when the weather is bad.

Calling for a taxi should get you a ride within 30 minutes, but few (if any) taxi companies handle calls in English. There'll also be an extra fee of around ¥500 tacked on to your fare.

Taxi Etiquette

When you've found your taxi, do <u>not</u> open the door. The driver controls it from his seat, and he'll open and close it for you when you get in and out of the cab. Avoid opening and closing the door yourself, unless you're trying to irritate your driver.

Some Tokyo cabbies speak English better than their New York counterparts, but you shouldn't expect this. If you have a map of where you want to go, you can reduce the potential for language trouble.

Fares

As of May 26, 1992, ¥600 gets you a base of 2 km, except after 11:00pm, when you get only 1.5 km. After your base distance, your charge is ¥90 for every 347 meters, or every 273 meters after 11:00pm. There are alternate fees for time spent stuck in traffic jams and slow-downs, so the fare from point A to point B can vary depending on how long you're standing still. On the bright side, you aren't expected to tip. It could be a very nice gesture, but it's not expected.

If you need a receipt, just ask. Your driver's receipt printer is linked to the meter, and it prints a receipt automatically when the driver hits the "total" button.

If you forget something in a cab (see p. 21), or if you want to file a complaint against a driver, call Kindaika Center's Taxi Hotline at 03-3648-0300. If you don't get the driver's name from his ID card, give them the taxi number from the side of the car or from your receipt.

How Can I Get a License to Drive in Japan?

What? You want to drive in Japan? But... why? You like narrow, confusing streets with bikes and pedestrians darting out in front of you? Road signs that you can't read? Traffic jams full of "Sunday drivers" that stretch for kilometers on end? Cars circling parking lots like vultures, waiting for a space to open up?

Well, maybe you're tired of walking everywhere. Maybe you'd feel freer on the open road than crammed into your train or subway. Maybe you'd like to go places and do things after the trains stop running. Maybe you've got a point.

Transferring Your License to a Japanese One

The easiest way to get a Japanese driver's license is to have your foreign license transferred to a Japanese one. To do this, you have to go to one of the following Driver's License Testing Centers.

1) Samezu Driver's License Testing Center (Samezu Unten Menkyo Shikenjo, or Samezu Shikenjo)

03-3474-1374

A 12 minute walk due east from the Keihin Tohoku line's Samezu Station, or a short bus ride from JR's Shinagawa Station. Take the bus for Oi Keibajo to Shikenjo-mae.

2) Koto Driver's License Testing Center (Koto Unten Menkyo Shikenjo, or Koto Shikenjo)   03-3699-1151

Take the Tozai line to Toyocho. It's about a five minute walk east. The Koto office is easy to reach if you live on the Chiba side of Tokyo.

3) Fuchu Driver's License Testing Center (Fuchu Unten Menkyo Shikenjo, or Fuchu Shikenjo)   0423-62-3591

The Fuchu center is really out of your way unless you live on the west side of Tokyo. Take the Keio line from Shinjuku to Tama-reien, then the bus for Tamamachi to Shikenjo-mae. Or take the Chuo line from Shinjuku to Musashi-koganei, then the #82 or #83 bus to Shikenjo-seimon-mae.

Applications are accepted at each center 8:30am to 4:00pm Monday through Friday.

At any testing center you need:

    1) your license issued in your home country

    2) your passport

    3) your Alien Registration Certificate

    4) a 3×2.4cm photo

There is a fee of about ¥3,200 for the transfer.

Who Can Answer My Questions About Visas in English?

The Tokyo Regional Immigration Bureau can answer questions about visas and immigration related matters by telephone in English, French and Chinese. However, these services are in great demand. Getting your call through can be quite difficult. The services for French and Chinese are limited to one day per week, and the services for all languages are from 9:30am to noon, and 1:00pm to 3:30pm.

In English   03-3213-8523 and 03-3213-8527
        Monday through Friday
In French   03-3214-5522
        Thursdays only
In Chinese   03-3214-5522
Officially, Tuesdays only, but sometimes more often

The Tokyo Metropolitan Government's Foreign Residents' Advisory Center can answer questions and give advice in several languages about a number of matters, not just visa issues.

In English   03-5320-7744
        Monday through Friday
In French   03-5320-7755
        Thursdays only
In Chinese   03-5320-7766
        Tuesdays and Fridays

<u>In Korean</u>   03-5320-7700
                  Wednesdays only
    The hours for each service are from 9:30am to noon,
and 1:00 to 4:00pm.

    The Japan Helpline can also answer questions or con-
nect you with people who can answer inquiries about
many concerns of daily life in Japan, including visas and
visa requirements.
    The Japan Helpline   0120-46-1997
                  Toll free, 24 hours

When Do I Need a Re-entry Permit and How Do I Get One?

If you are in Japan with a visa and you plan to leave the country temporarily, you need a re-entry permit. Without one, the visa you have when you leave Japan will <u>not</u> be valid on your return, and you'll have to go through the hoops again for a new one.

Applications for re-entry permits are available at all immigration offices. If the office is not crowded, getting a permit can take as little as thirty minutes.

There are two types of re-entry permits: single re-entry permits, which allow you to leave and return to Japan once under your current visa status, and multiple re-entry permits, which allow you to come and go freely. Both types are valid either for one year after your receive the permit, or until your visa expires, whichever comes first. The fees are ¥3,000 for a single re-entry permit, and ¥6,000 for a multiple.

Common sense says that if you're going to spend the time applying, get the multiple. However, immigration officials have the final say on which one you're going to get, and if you can't justify your request for a multiple re-entry permit you may have to make do with a single.

To get either type of re-entry permit you need:
1) A completed application form
2) Your Alien Registration Certificate
3) Your passport
4) Cash (for the fees above)

If you hold a short-term visa (under 90 days), you are not eligible for a re-entry permit.

Immigration

The Tokyo Regional Immigration Bureau has three offices in the metropolitan region. Given the number of foreigners in the region, you might suspect that the system is pushed to its limits, and you'd be right. Getting a re-entry permit usually doesn't take too much time, but many other immigration services (for example, changing your visa status or renewing your visa) can keep you waiting for a long time. Think of it as a chance to catch up on your reading or letter writing, but don't let the wait get to you and do <u>not</u> take your frustrations out on an immigration official. The staff is all too aware that there are only three immigration offices in the area, and they probably aren't too happy with their work load either. Also, Japan's "case-by-case" style of immigration control means that the officer handling your case has a lot of influence in whatever decision is reached.

Don't do anything stupid.

The Tokyo Regional Immigration Bureau's main office is in Otemachi, which is on the Marunouchi, Tozai, Chiyoda, Hanzomon, and Toei Mita lines. Take exit C-2, the office is about two minutes from the station. They oversee immigration matters in Tokyo and nine surrounding prefectures. They're busy.

Tokyo Regional Immigration Bureau   03-3213-8111

The Hakozaki Branch Office, located in the Tokyo City Air Terminal (TCAT), is said to be a lot faster than

Otemachi. To check for yourself, go to Suitengu-mae, the last (or first) stop on the Hanzomon line. About two minutes from Exit 1.

Hakozaki Branch Office   **03-3665-7157**

If you live in the Yokohama area your closest office is the Yokohama Immigration Bureau. Take the Keihin Tohoku or Tokyu Toyoko line to Sakuragicho, then bus #58 or #8 to Yamashita Goto Chosha Yokohama Chihou Godochosha-mae.

Yokohama Immigration Bureau   **045-681-6801**

In general, the earlier you get to immigration the faster you'll be processed out. If things are really busy, there may be a cut-off time after which applications are no longer distributed so the staff can finish up on schedule.

3 You and Your Money

How Should I Choose a Bank?

Japan has one central bank, eleven city banks, 64 first tier regional banks, 66 second tier regional banks, 87 foreign banks, three long-term credit banks, 440 credit associations, 372 credit cooperatives and a number of other financial institutions. There's a lot to choose from.

You're under enough pressure in a foreign culture without worries about your bank or your money. Convenience is everything, and the most convenient banks are the ones with the most branches. These are the city banks, and they are probably your best bet for banking in Japan. They work together in the BANCS system (see p. 84), and you can make deposits and withdrawals with automatic teller machines (ATMs) and cash dispensers (CDs) at most any of the network's 3,267 branches in Japan.

Each has its own individual touches, but a bank is a bank and the city banks are all quite similar to one another. The determining factor is most cases is location. The best bank for you has branches near your home and workplace, but other considerations can influence your choice of banks. Would you like a "Hello Kitty" (Mitsubishi Bank), an "Ahirunopekkle" (Fuji Bank), or a "Snoopy" (Sanwa Bank) bankbook? And which is the proper bankbook for the aspiring foreign businessperson in Japan? Which bank conjures up more "Japanese" images - Fuji Bank or Sakura Bank? Do you want a bank that operates on a global scale, or would you rather stick with a smaller regional bank?

Banks are certainly not your only options. Services offered at your local post office are comparable to those of the city banks, and the interest on postal savings accounts is often a bit more generous. The post offices have a nationwide network of some 11,600 ATMs and CDs, but their weekend services are more limited than those of the city banks.

Regional banks and *shinkin* banks (credit associations) are locally based, which means they have fewer branches than the city banks, but that doesn't always mean a smaller bank won't do the job. If you work near your home you'll only need one or two places to bank, not 3,267.

How Do I Open a Bank Account?

Opening a bank account is a lot easier in Japan than in some other countries. There isn't so much trouble with the procedures here as with the language - "I want to open an account" is pretty tough to communicate through gestures alone.

If you're in a larger bank you'll probably be met by someone in a bank uniform and escorted to the "New Accounts" window or to a ticket machine, which will give you a number corresponding to your place in line.

When your number comes up you'll get the big banking smile and an application form from the people across the counter. Take the form back to the waiting area and fill it out there. When you finish, give it back to them in a break between customers. They'll ask to see your Alien Registration Certificate and they'll make sure you filled in the "secret number" part of the application for your cash card. When you open an account you need to make a symbolic deposit - any amount will do - so they'll ask about that, too. Opening an account is not very difficult, but be careful when they ask to make a print of your *inkan*, or name seal.

The Inkan vs Your Signature

Where most foreigners use a signature to prove their identity, Japanese use their name seal, or *inkan*. You, a foreigner, probably don't have an *inkan*, and your signature is as meaningful to most Japanese institutions as their inkan is to you: it looks like a bunch of squiggles that <u>anyone</u> could copy or forge. But banks will usually let you open an account with your signature if you don't have an *inkan*. The catch in many cases is that you also have to remember <u>another</u> secret number - this one for any transactions you might make at the window.

If you're aware of this, fine, no problem. But if you forget the window number you can run into trouble. For example, if you lose your cash card, or if you manage to erase the magnetic strip on it, you can't use an ATM or CD until your card is fixed or replaced. But if you go to the window to ask for a new card, how will you prove you're really who you say you are? After all, you don't have an inkan. All you have are a lot of funny squiggles that anyone could copy or forge. If your bank has the "signature-plus-secret-window-number system", write down your secret window number and keep it in a safe place whether or not you ever plan to make a window transaction. If you have an *inkan*, they will make one print of it for their records and put another in your bankbook. You'll need to have the *inkan* with you to make certain window transactions - to close your account, for example. The bank staff will compare the seal you put on the transaction request with the one in their records to see if they match.

After you've dealt with this, choose what style bankbook you want (some banks let you choose your cash card as well), and the attendant will record your deposit in it. You will usually receive your bankbook the day you apply, but preparations for the cash card take a week or two. You can ask the bank to mail it to you or you can go by and pick it up yourself. It will be sent by registered mail if you have it mailed, so if you're not home when the postman comes, you can pick it up at the post office.

Are Japanese banks really happy to have your money? Banks in some countries give toaster ovens, blankets, flashlights and the like to new accountholders. Japanese banks give you boxes of tissues.

How Do I Make Deposits and Withdrawals with ATMs and CDs?

Banker's Hours

Account opened, cash card in hand, you're ready to withdraw some cash. But will the bank let you? In defiance of Western notions of automated banking, 24-hour cash service has yet to reach Japan. There are explanations, but they don't remedy the inconvenience.

The cash dispensers (CDs) and automatic teller machines (ATMs) of most major banks are open for business from 8:45am to 7:00pm Monday through Friday, and from 9:00am to 5:00pm on Saturdays and Sundays. Some branches don't have Sunday service at all, while some are open to 6:00pm. There are also extra fees charged for transactions made at certain times on certain days.

The BANCS Network

One plus for ATMs is that if your bank is a member of the BANCS network, you can make withdrawals at any other member bank for a small service charge.

	Monday-Friday 8:45am-6:00pm (after 6:00pm)	Saturday 9:00am-2:00pm (after 2:00pm)	Sunday
Your bank (all branches)	No charge (¥103)	No charge (¥103)	¥103
Other BANCS members	¥103 (¥206)	¥103 (¥206)	¥206

Eleven banks participate in the BANCS network. They are: Asahi Bank (formerly Kyowa Saitama Bank), Dai-ichi Kangyo Bank, Daiwa Bank, Fuji Bank, Hokkaido Takushoku Bank, Mitsubishi Bank, Sakura Bank (formerly Mitsui Taiyo Kobe Bank), Sanwa Bank, Sumitomo Bank, Tokai Bank, and Bank of Tokyo.

Making a Withdrawal

Dai-ichi Kangyo Bank's ATMs can take you through all their functions in English if you select the "English Guidance" service. Unfortunately, they are the only bank with this service. Other banks usually have booklets in English explaining the uses and fees of their machines.

To make a withdrawal from the typical ATM or CD

1) Touch the button marked 払戻し or 引き出し.

2) Insert your card as shown in illustrations on the machine.

3) Enter your secret number. The machine will return your card to you if you enter a wrong number, and if you enter a wrong number three times it may void or keep your card.

4) How much money do you want to withdraw? The character 万 stands for 10,000, and the character 千 for 1,000. If you want ¥84,000, it's best to push 8, 万, 4, 千, then 円, the character for yen. If you change your mind or make a mistake, press 訂正 or ✕ and enter your correction. When you correctly enter the amount you want, press はい or ◯. You can enter 84, 千, but you may end up with 84 one-thousand yen bills.

5) The machine will whir and hum a while, then return your card to you. Next, a small door will open and you can take your cash. Most machines will also give you a

transaction slip for your records, or mark your withdrawal in your bankbook. (Depending on the machine, you can also have the transaction recorded in you bankbook if you insert it into the machine when you insert your card.

If you think you've made a mistake or if you're having trouble with the machine, press the cancel button (取消 or ✕), and start again.

Most banks have an attendants stationed near the machines to take care of people having trouble, so don't be afraid to ask for help if you're not seeing eye-to-eye with the machine.

There is probably an alarm or "panic button" near the ATM as well. This alerts the police to trouble in the bank and will bring them there right away. Use it only in an emergency.

Making a Deposit

It's easier to put money into your account than it is to take it out. Depending on your bank, you may only need your bankbook to make a deposit. Most cash dispensers are limited to dispensing cash, so you need to use an ATM to make deposits.

The procedure is usually something like

1) Push the button marked 入金 or 預金.

2) Insert your card and/or your bankbook in the proper slots.

3) Put your bills in the slot that opens next. It helps to have the bills lined up and stacked neatly.

4) The door will close and the amount you're depositing will be shown on the screen. If the amount is correct, push はい, or ○. If the amount is incorrect, push 訂正, or ✕, and try again.

5) After the machine credits your account with the deposit, it will return your updated bankbook, and/or your card and a transaction slip.

As with making a withdrawal, don't hesitate to ask the attendants for help. It's their job. They'll figure out what the trouble is whether or not you speak the same language.

ATMs differ from CDs in that with CDs you can only withdraw money (or in some cases make transfers with your card). With ATMs you can make deposits and withdrawals and transfers. The steps above work on both ATMs and CDs.

How Can I Pay Bills at a Bank or Post Office?

By and large, Japanese don't pay bills with checks. They ask a bank, a post office, or in some cases a convenience store to transfer money into the other party's bank account. The type of bills you can pay at a convenience store is limited (see p. 96), but you can pay most any bill at a bank or post office. The catch with banks is most of them are only open for a few moments on weekdays and not at all on weekends.

Transfers are divided into window transfers, ATM transfers (see p. 90), and automatic transfers (see p. 125). For general purposes, window transfers with cash are the easiest, because all you do is fill in a transfer form (*furikomi iraisho*) and hand over the money. For some bills at post offices and some banks, all you need to do is turn in the bill and your money.

Most banks have different forms for general transfers and for transfers to pay utilities. Some banks don't require forms at all for utility bills. Fill in the form you need as in the example below. Write only within the fat lines. You don't need to use kanji, but katakana and hiragana are preferred to the alphabet. If you sending money to a foreigner, make sure you know what his/her name is in katakana. Does James Brown become *Jeemusu Buraun* or *Jeemuzu Buraun?*

Put the transfer form and your money in the plastic tray

88

at the window, then head off to the waiting area. Go to the counter when they call you again, and they'll give you a receipt and your change.

Below is a sample *furikomi iraisho* for general transfers.

A) The first five katakana characters of the recipient's bank

B) The first five katakana characters of the recipient's bank branch

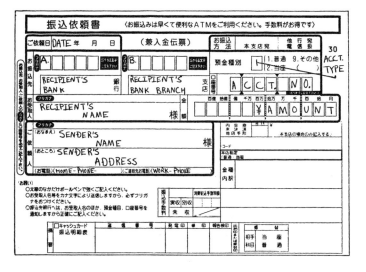

How Can I Pay Bills with an ATM?

If you can't make it to the bank between 9:00am and 3:00pm, or if you don't have the time to wait in line to make a transfer at the window, you can pay many of your bills with the ATM.

With the ATM you can send cash and make transfers outside normal banking hours. If you're sending cash, you can send it from almost any bank in Japan, whether or not you have an account.

Many people hesitate to use the ATM, but there's no reason to be afraid. It only does what you tell it to do, and there are enough safeguards and chances to stop along the way so that you can end a transaction whenever you think it's gotten out of hand. Once you are comfortable with the ATM's system you can save a lot of time.

How To Pay Your Bills With The ATM

Each bank's system has its own particulars, but all are basically the same. You can make a cash transfer from almost any bank in Japan, but you should use your bank or a bank that cooperates with yours if you're transferring cash directly from your account to another.

As of yet, Dai-ichi Kangyo is the only bank to take you through ATM functions in English. Below is a general guide to ATM functions for someone making a cash transfer.

1. Choose the characters below from the main menu.

振込　or　振り込み

The characters are read *furikomi*, and they mean "money transfer".

2. Next, choose what kind of transfer you want to make. In this example we're sending cash to pay the rent, so we want "cash transfer", or *genkin furikomi* as below.

現金振込　or　現金振り込み

3. Now tell the ATM who you want to send your money to, what bank, etc., usually in the order below. Match the information about the recipient with the characters and answer when asked.

A. 銀行

What bank does the recipient use?

B. 支店

What branch of the bank does the recipient use?

C. 預金種別

What kind of account does the recipient have? Choose

普通　or　当座

(The first choice is more common)

D. 口座番号

What is the recipient's account number?

E. お受取人　(Anything with 受取)

Who (or what company) is going to receive your money? Choose the characters below it you want to use the alphabct.

英字

Variations: Some machines ask you to input the names for A and B in katakana. Other machines display all the katakana and ask you to choose the character the bank or branch begins with, then switch to a screen of all banks that start with that character. For example, under the katakana heading "da" you would find Dai-ichi Kangyo Bank and Daiwa Bank, under "sa" would be Sanwa Bank and Sakura Bank, etc. The branch names can be listed this way as well, with the Tahata, Tamagawa, and Tama-reien branches of XXX bank all under "ta". Charts of both Japanese writing systems, hiragana and katakana, are included with their English readings in the appendix.

Some machines ask you to confirm or change (see below) after every entry in **3.** Some wait until you've entered all the above information.

4. Next, you usually have a chance to confirm, change or erase altogether the information you've entered so far.

A.　　　確認

"Confirm" (*Kakunin*) Press this when everything is in order and no changes are necessary.

B.　　　訂正　or　変更

"Change" (*Teisei* or *henkou*) Press this if you need to change something. Select which area from **3** you need to correct and go back to it. After you make a correction, you usually start back at the beginning of this section.

C.　　　取消　or　取り消す

(*Torikesu*) This is the "cancel" button. If you want to start all over again at the very beginning, or if you've had enough of ATMs for one day, choose this. You will usually be asked to confirm this decision, which means you'll need **4A** or **4B** again, or "yes" and "no".

yes	○	はい
no	✕	いいえ

5. Next, you need to provide some information about yourself. You are requesting the bank to transfer your money to another person's account, so you are represented by the characters for "person making request", or

A.　　ご依頼人　or　依頼人

> Enter your name the way you entered the recipient's name in **3E**. Remember that you can use the alphabet if you want.

Next, enter your telephone number after

B.　　電話番号

> Either your home number or your work number will do. If the bank has trouble processing your transfer, they'll call you and straighten it out.

6. The next screen will ask you to confirm the data about yourself, as you did in **4** above.

7. The next screen will show the amount of money you're sending and the handling fee the bank will charge. The fee varies with the bank you're using, the bank the recipient is using, the amount you're sending and other details.

As before, you'll have a chance to confirm or change

the amount you're sending, or to cancel the transaction altogether as in **4.**

8. Finally, you get one more chance to confirm everything. All the information on your transaction will be on the screen, so check over everything once again and decide as in **4** to confirm <u>everything</u> or change something.

9. After you confirm everything once more, the machine asks how you are going to pay for the transfer.

A.   紙幣と硬貨

"Bills and coins" (*Shihei to kouka*) This means you can unload your change on the ATM, but most machines can only handle a certain number of coins at one time.

B.   紙幣のみ

"Bills only" (*Shihei nomi*) Unlike payphones, ATMs will give you change.

If you pay in both bills and coins, two doors will open. Put the bills in the drawer marked *shihei* (with the characters above), and the coins in the *kouka* drawer.

After you put your money in, the doors will close and the ATM will whir and click as it sorts your money and information. If everything checks out, the ATM will give you your change and print up a receipt for you. Some banks have special record books, different from the bankbook of deposits and withdrawals, for keeping track of your transfers. If you don't have one of these books, or if you're transferring cash from a bank at which you don't have an account, <u>keep the receipt</u>. It is proof that you paid your bill.

As a cute touch, many ATMs will display cartoon

characters bowing to you after you complete a transaction. After the bowing, the screen should go back to the initial menu in **1.**

There is almost always a bank employee assigned to the ATM area to take care of people having trouble with the machines. If the ATM isn't doing what you want it to do, don't hesitate to ask the attendant for help.

What Bills Can I Pay at Convenience Stores?

If you work nine to five in a country that doesn't use checks and that has banking hours of nine to three, how do you pay your bills? ATMs can do the job, but their hours don't always match yours. Plus, you have to deal with the machines. What other ways can you pay your bills?

Enter the convenience store and the bar code. Despite the bar code's unmatched ugliness and the convenience store's lack of charm, the two of them combine to make paying some bills very easy.

You can pay most of your utility bills at convenience stores. One notable exception to this is your water bill, but water bills only come every two months. If a utility bill has a bar code on it, you can pay it according to the chart below. If the bill does not have a bar code on it, you can't pay it at a convenience store.

	Electricity	Gas	NHK	NTT	KDD	JT	DDI
Seven-Eleven	X	X	X	X	X	X	X
Lawson	X	X	X	X	X	X	X
Family Mart	X	X	X	X	X	X	X
Ministop	X	X	X				X
Sun Chain	X	X	X	X	X	X	
Yamazaki Daily Store	X	X	X	X			
SunEvery	X	X	X	X			
Sunkus	X	X	X				

When your bill comes in the mail, head to your convenience store. Walk in, set the bill on the counter, pay, get your receipt and leave. You don't need to say a word. There is no extra fee for using the convenience store, so the amount on the bill is the amount you pay.

Don't wad up or fold your bill. When you give the bill to the clerks they'll read its bar code, then stamp it with the store's seal. They'll give you the stamped part of the bill and a receipt from the register. If you need to prove you paid the bill, the stamped half of the bill should be proof enough, but it can't hurt to keep both.

Utilities bills and the convenience store's merchandise are rung up using different systems, so they're rung up on different receipts. Also, each utility company is on a different system, so if you pay your phone, gas and electricity bills at once, you'll get three receipts.

How Do I Pay My Taxes in Japan?

In most cases your employer in Japan will withhold your income taxes (*shotoku-zei*) automatically and pay them for you. At the end of the year they'll match what you should pay with what they've deducted and adjust things from there.

In Tokyo, you also pay Tokyo Metropolitan resident's taxes (*Tomin-zei*) and resident's taxes for your ward or city (*Kumin-zei* or *Shimin-zei*). It's best to check whether or not your employer is withholding these as well, because if not you'll get the bill in the mail. It's not good to get bills that big out of the blue.

At the end of the tax year and after your employer has deducted everything and made the proper adjustments (giving you a refund or taking a little more) you should receive your *Gensen-choushuu-hyou*. This is the equivilent of the W-2 form in the U.S., showing your income and the amount deducted from it for various taxes. You can be asked to produce the *Gensen-choushuu-hyou* at odd times, particularly in dealings with the immigration bureau.

Who Can I Call for Information on My Japanese Taxes?

The Tokyo Regional Tax Bureau can, as you might expect, field your questions about Japanese taxes. They accept inquiries in English from 9:00am to 5:00pm Monday through Friday at 03-3216-6811.

Additionally, the Tokyo Metropolitan Government's Foreign Residents' Advisory Center (see p. 74) can answer your questions or put you in touch with people who can.

Taxes for My Home Country

If your home country's tax authorities haven't found you, it may be a good idea to get in touch with them, as tax laws for overseas nationals vary from country to country. American citizens, for example, are required to file tax returns on income earned in Japan. Income earned here is already taxed by the Japanese government, so the U.S. gives an exemption of up to $70,000 on this if you meet certain requirements. Still, you can't get the exemption unless you file a return.

If, somehow, the Internal Revenue Service doesn't know where you are, you can write them care of the embassy and they'll send you Overseas Filers Of Form 1040, an 82 page booklet of forms and explanations to help you answer everything.

Check with your legation. If you don't, it <u>can</u> come back to haunt you.

How Can I Send Money Overseas?

There are two ways to send money overseas from Japan.
1) From Banks
   a) In-payment to the recipient's bank account
   b) Demand drafts
2) From Post Offices
   a) Transfers from one giro account to another
   b) In-payment to the recipient's giro account
   c) In-payment to the recipient's bank account
   d) International postal money orders

International Remittance From Banks

In-payment to the recipient's bank account by telegraphic transfer is the safest and fastest way to send money abroad, but it's also the most expensive. You give your money to a bank, and they cable or telex it to the recipient's bank. You need the recipient's name and address, his bank's name and branch name (and address to be safe), and his account number.

If you don't have the recipient's account information, you can use the "advise and pay" method, in which the bank notifies the recipient that you have sent him some money. He can then pick up the money at his convenience.

With a telegraphic transfer you pay the telex/cable fee and a commission to the sending bank. The recipient may also pay a fee. Your cost will be in the ¥4,000-¥7,000 range.

Banks also offer in-payment via postal transfer, which means the transfer is sent by the postal system rather than electronic means. Naturally, postal transfers take longer to reach the recipient than telegraphic transfers. The fees total in the ¥3,000-¥4,000 range. This service is not very popular.

Demand drafts are the cheapest of the three, but they are slower than the others and not as safe. You give the bank your money and they give you a draft (minus a ¥2,000-¥3,000 commission), which you yourself mail to the recipient. The recipient then cashes the draft at a bank.

If you send more than ¥5,000,000, you are required to file a report with the Ministry of Finance.

Not all banks can send money overseas. Banks that handle international transfers advertise the fact with "Authorized Foreign Exchange Bank" or "AFEB" signs near their entrances. Additionally, some branches of smaller banks take longer to send or issue demand drafts than major banks.

Postal Remittance

Japan's larger post offices also offer several overseas remittance services, including direct transfers to bank accounts and postal giro accounts. In fact, the least expensive way to send money overseas is to use a giro transfer from your postal account to the recipient's. The trouble with this system is that the transfers are only from one giro account to another, and some countries, notably the U.S., don't use giro accounts. If you don't have a giro account but your recipient does, you can send money as an in-payment and pay a fee of ¥700 to ¥1,500.

Overseas Remittance to Giro Accounts

Remittance	Charges	
	In-payment	Transfer
Up to ¥100,000	¥700	
¥100,001-200,000	¥1,000	¥400
¥200,001-500,000	¥1,500	

An additional ¥500 fee is added to the ¥1,500 figure for every ¥500,000 or part thereof over the initial ¥500,000.

Post offices also sell international postal money orders, which you mail directly to the recipient, similar to the demand draft service from banks mentioned above. The recipient cashes the money order at his post office. With international postal money orders, the amount you pay in yen is converted to the recipient's currency at the exchange rate on the date of remittance.

Fees for International Postal Money Orders

Remittance	Charges
Up to ¥100,000	¥1,000
¥100,001-200,000	¥1,500
¥200,001-500,000	¥2,000

An additional ¥500 fee is added to the ¥2,000 figure for every ¥500,000 or part thereof after the initial ¥500,000. ¥500 is subtracted from the above fees for sending remittance directly to the U.S.

Postal transfers and in-payments to Germany, France, the U.K., Korea and the U.S. take six to ten days to complete, and transfers to Canada, Australia and the Philippines take between 20 and 30 days.

If you're in a hurry, you can send remittance by telegraph or telex. This service is only available to certain countries, and you must pay additional fees of ¥4,400 for remittance by telegram, or ¥1,000 by telex. Whether the remittance is by telegram or telex varies from country to country.

4 Services and Utilities

How Can I Use Public Telephones? How Can I Use Them for International Calls?

A domestic call from a public telephone is one of Japan's best bargains, as a three minute call within the 23 wards costs only ¥10. The basics of using a payphone in Japan are the same as in most other countries, but there are a few differences to remember. To use a payphone, lift the receiver and insert your coins or telephone card. When you hear the tone, dial your call. However, if you hear a "beep" during your conversation, your time is up. Put in another coin or phone card <u>or you will be disconnected</u>.

The payphone will return any unused change when you put down the receiver, but no change will be returned from a ¥100 coin. If you make a ¥20 call with a ¥100 coin, the difference will not be returned and you're out ¥80. One way to get around this is to keep a pocketful of ¥10 coins wherever you go. A more practical idea is to use a telephone card. Telephone cards are prepaid cards that can only be used for phone calls. Telephone cards can be used at green payphones, green payphones with gold plates, and digital (black) payphones. If the small red light on the upper left of a payphone is not lit, the phone will not accept telephone cards and you have to use coins. Some versions of the green payphone accept telephone cards <u>only</u>. Telephone cards come in a variety of designs and are sold at kiosks, convenience stores and other shops, as well as vending machines.

Red, pink, and yellow payphones can only be used for calls within Japan, and some red and pink payphones only accept ¥10 coins. Digital phones and green phones with gold plates on the front can be used for international calls, but other green payphones without gold plates cannot.

International Calls from Payphones

International calls from payphones are calculated in ¥100 units, so to call overseas from a payphone, you must insert a ¥100 coin or a telephone card with at least ¥100 credit. Placing an international call from a payphone is the same as dialing international from a private phone. You can dial direct by choosing a service (IDC 0061, ITJ 0041, or KDD 001), then the country code, area code and local number. Paying for your call was easy when NTT sold ¥5,000 telephone cards, but too many counterfeit cards turned up and NTT banned the card. The highest denomination card on the market today is ¥1,000.

You can use KDD's Home Country Direct and IDC's Country Direct (see p. 109) from payphones the same way you use them from private phones. There is no extra fee for using either service from a payphone.

KDD offers the only operator-assisted services, so credit card or collect calls that are not placed through Home Country Direct or Country Direct must be placed through the KDD operator. Dial 0051 for operator-assisted calls.

How Do I Get a Phone Connection?

You can buy or rent a phone line, depending on how much you want to spend and how long you're planning to stay in Japan. If you're not going to be in Japan too long, a rented line is the more economical option, but a major drawback is that often with a rented line you can't make or receive international calls.

There are a number of companies that rent phone lines, and many real estate agencies act as brokers for rental companies. Many rental companies require deposits and/or Japanese guarantors. The deposits are usually refundable, but make sure before you sign anything.

If buying a line is the way you want to go, contact your local NTT office by dialing 116, or call NTT Information at 03-3277-1010. They'll direct you to the NTT office nearest you.

Buying a phone line costs a whopping ¥72,000, with another ¥800 for a contract fee and ¥2,184 worth of consumption tax to total ¥74,984. The total must be paid before NTT sends a work crew to connect your service. One small plus is that you can often choose your phone number from a list of three or four options. Installation costs about ¥12,000.

As for the telephone itself, you can buy or rent one from NTT, or you can buy one somewhere else. Discount shops usually have the best deals.

Another ugly thing about buying a line from NTT is that NTT will not buy it back when you leave the country. Fortunately, there are groups that will buy the rights to your line for a decent price.

Individuals can sell the rights to their phone lines, and this can be a good way to buy a line for less than the going rate. Check the classified ads in the local English language newspapers and see what's there. To buy a line from or to sell your line to an individual, you need to take care of some paperwork at your local NTT office. Call NTT Information for details.

How Can I Make International Calls?

All international calls go through ITJ, IDC, or KDD. Their fees are all about the same, and their discount hours, covered below, are identical. The only service to allow you to make operator-assisted calls from Japan (person-to-person, credit card, etc.) is KDD. In most cases you can dial direct with any of the systems, but people living in some areas are required to register before using the services. Check by calling the information lines below.

The Big Three

ITJ (International Telecom Japan) has service to 52 areas around the world, including Australia, Canada, France, Germany, Hong Kong, Korea, Malaysia, New Zealand, the U.K., and the U.S.A. To use ITJ from any phone (for payphones, only black payphones and green ones with gold plates on the front can handle international calls) dial 0041, the country code, the area code, and the local number.

IDC (International Digital Communications) covers service with Belgium, Canada, China, Denmark, India, Korea, Mexico, Thailand, the U.K., the U.S.A., and 46 other areas. To use IDC, call 0061, the country code, the area code, and the local number. If you replace 0061 with 0062, IDC will let you know the charges for the call as soon as you hang up.

With IDC's Country Direct you can reach an operator in the country you're calling, then place a credit card or collect call directly. If you place a credit card call, the card must have been issued outside Japan. An advantage to the system is that you deal with operators only in the language of the country you're calling, and with credit card or collect calls you're not billed in Japan.

To use Country Direct, dial 0066-55, then the three digit access number of the country you're calling. Some of the access numbers are below. Call IDC's toll-free information line for more details and access numbers of other areas.

Country	Access Number
U.S.A. (ATT)	111
(USS)	877
U.K.	144
Hong Kong	852

KDD (001) covers almost every country in the world. Direct dialing is 001, country code, area code, and the local number.

Only KDD offers operator-assisted calls from Japan, which include person-to-person, station-to-station, credit card and collect calls. To make an operator-assisted call, dial 0051 and tell the operator what type of call you want to make.

KDD offers two other long distance services, Home Country Direct and Dial Coupon 001. Home Country Direct resembles IDC's Country Direct, and is also for collect and credit card calls. There are no extra charges for the service. To use Home Country Direct, dial 0039 plus the country's access number. The Home Country Direct access number is not the same as the country code, and

KDD's Home Country Direct access numbers are not the same as those of IDC's Country Direct.

Country	Access Number	Country	Access Number
U.S.A.	111 (ATT)	Canada	161
	121 (MCI)	Australia	611
	131 (USS)	New Zealand	641
Hawaii	181	Hong Kong	852
U.K.	441		

Call KDD's information line for access numbers of countries not listed above.

With Dial Coupon 001 you make a contract with KDD for 30, 60 or 90 minutes of international calls per month to a specific area, and you pay a fixed monthly rate. You can call as often as you like - the example KDD uses is for 30 one minute calls - as long as you don't go over the contracted time. There are some restrictions and more details, so call KDD for more information.

When to Call

ITJ, IDC and KDD all have the same discount-rate periods. The standard rate is Monday through Friday from 8:00am to 7:00pm Japan Time. Economy rates, 20 percent off the standard rates, are in effect weekdays from 7:00pm to 11:00pm, and from 8:00am to 11:00pm on weekends and holidays. Discount rates are 40 percent off the standard, and are every day from 11:00pm to 8:00am. Discount and economy rates are only valid for direct dialing.

Interestingly enough, no matter which service you use at what time, it's cheaper to call the U.S.- on the far side of the Pacific- than it is to call any of Japan's Asian neighbors except Korea.

KDD also has directory information for overseas telephone numbers. For more information call 0057.

Information on International Calls

ITJ	0120-440-041 (toll free)
IDC	0120-030-061 (toll free)
KDD	0057 (toll free)

Direct Dialing in Brief

ITJ	0041 + country code + area code + local number
IDC	0061 + country code + area code + local number
KDD	001 + country code + area code + local number

Operator Assisted Calls (KDD) 0051
Country Direct (IDC)   0066-55 + access number
Home Country Direct (KDD)   0039 + access number

What Other Telephone Services are Available?

NTT Information

NTT has an information line in English to help you with bills, hook-ups, moving and other services. The Tokyo number is 03-3277-1010, and the Yokohama number is 045-322-1010. Both offices are open from 9:00am to 5:00pm Monday through Friday.

Directory Service (Domestic)

You can get directory information on numbers in Japan by calling 104 and giving the operator the name and address of the person or group you're seeking. There is a ¥30 fee, and to use the service from a pay phone you must insert ¥30 or a phone card with ¥30 of credit or more remaining. The service is in Japanese only.

Domestic Collect Calls

International collect calls are discussed in the previous section, but domestic collect calls are another matter altogether. To place a collect call to a number within Japan dial 106, then give NTT your name and the number you wish to contact. The operator will call the other party and connect you if they accept the charges. There is a fee for using a "100" number, and a ¥90 charge for going through an operator.

Free Dial

Free dial numbers are toll free numbers, which means you are not charged for the call. The pattern for free dial numbers is 0120 followed by six digits.

Dial Q2 (0990)

The opposite of the free dial number is the dial Q2 number. By calling a dial Q2 number you agree to pay a certain fee for the time you stay on the line. Naturally, the longer you're on the line the higher your bill is going to be.

The service is used by many information lines, for example, the latest sports updates or the most recent foreign exchange rates. It's also the number for all the girly cards you find in phone booths.

Dial Q2 numbers are 0990 followed by six digits.

Other Numbers

There are special 100 numbers for weather updates and forecasts (177), as well as the exact time (117). Unfortunatcly, both these services are in Japanese only.

To report telephone service problems, dial 113. Though if the trouble with your phone is severe you may need to use a payphone.

You can make calls to someone on a *shinkansen* (bullet train) by dialing 107. You need to know the line and train the person you're calling is on.

Domestic Information	104
Calls To Shinkansen	107
Telephone Service Problems	113
Exact Time	117
Weather Updates and Forecasts	177

What are the Rules and Rates for Postal Service?

Domestic Mail

A standard-size letter-type item (14-23.5cm long, 9-12cm wide and up to 1cm thick) 25g or less in weight can be sent to any address in Japan for ¥62. Standard-size letter-type items over 25g but under 50g need ¥72 stamps. Postcards can be sent for ¥41.

Hours

Post offices are open as follows:

	Monday-Friday	Saturday	Sundays/Holidays
Delivery Post Offices	9:00am-7:00pm (9:00am-5:00pm at some offices)	9:00am-5:00pm	Closed (9:00am-12:30 at some offices)
Non-delivery Post Offices	9:00am-5:00pm	Closed	Closed

Delivery post offices are the larger post offices that collect and distribute mail. Non-delivery post offices are the smaller local post offices that only collect mail. Both types handle savings and insurance matters.

Seasonal and Prepaid Postcards

Nengajou and *nengahagaki* (New Year's letters and postcards) are far more popular in Japan than Xmas cards.

Most *nengajou* have lottery numbers on them, with many different prizes available. The most common prizes are sheets of commemorative stamps, and the winning numbers are published in newspapers and posted at the post office. If you have a winning number, you can claim your prize at any post office. It's nice to let the person who sent you the winning card know his or her card was lucky.

Greetings postcards for summer (Kamo-mail) and other occasions are also common, but not as popular as *nengajou*.

If you make a mistake when writing a prepaid postcard, you can exchange it at the post office for a new one for a ¥5 fee.

Registered Mail and Sending Cash

You can send items via registered mail by asking for *kakitome* at the counter. If you mail cash within Japan, ask at the counter for a *genkin kakitome fuutou* and you'll get a special cash registration envelope. You can send a letter along with your money. If something happens to your money in a cash registration envelope, the Ministry of Posts and Telecommunications will pay you the amount you sent up to ¥500,000. If, however, you fail to write the amount sent in the proper space on the outside of the envelope, the most you're covered for is ¥10,000.

Express Mail

You can send items by express if you make a red horizontal line along the upper right part of your letter. The service is available all over Japan. There is an extra fee, so if you're not sure how much the express charge will cost, ask at the post office window for *sokutatsu*.

Change of Address

If you move within Japan, your mail will be forwarded to you if you fill out a change of address form. Domestic mail and letter and postcard-type international mail will be forwarded free of charge, but the post office will add a charge for forwarding international parcels. If you move overseas, items sent from within Japan to your old address in Japan will not be forwarded to your overseas address, so it might be a good idea to have your mail forwarded to a friend in Japan. To get a change of address form, ask at your post office for a *tenkyo todoke*.

The post office recommends you turn in a *tenkyo todoke* when you first move to Japan, so they know where you are when your mail catches up with you.

Designated Delivery Date

You can designate the date of delivery for domestic mail for an extra ¥20 for letter-type items and ¥50 for parcels. This is helpful when sending birthday or anniversary letters and the like.

International Mail

International mail in Japan generally falls under the following four categories: letter-type post, parcel post, EMS and INTELPOST. Letter-post is divided into letters (including aerogrammes), postcards, printed matter, small packets and literature for the blind. You can send letter-post and parcel post items by surface mail, SAL (surface airlifted) or airmail.

Surface mail is the slowest, and for parcel post, usually

the least expensive. Write "SURFACE" on any item you want sent by surface mail.

SAL is less expensive than airmail, but faster than surface mail. With SAL, your letter or package goes largely via air, but it waits on a space-available basis. You can send items to about 60 countries around the world in two to three weeks. Put a SAL sticker on the upper left face of the addressed side of the item, or write "SAL" there.

For airmail service, write "AIRMAIL" or "PAR AVION" on the item you're sending. Sample rates are below.

20kg package to	Surface	SAL	Airmail
Australia	¥8,400	¥19,100	¥29,600
N. America	¥11,150	¥18,900	¥25,500
U.K.	¥9,050	¥20,200	¥29,700
10kg package to			
Australia	¥5,400	¥12,100	¥18,600
N. America	¥7,150	¥11,900	¥16,500
U.K.	¥6,050	¥13,200	¥18,700

Express mail (*sokutatsu*) and registered mail (*kakitome*) services are also available for international mail. The fees are ¥300 and ¥450 for express international letter-post items and parcel post respectively, and ¥350 for registered letters.

You can also confirm that mail has been delivered to the addressee, though this service is not available for uninsured parcels to all countries. The fee for advice of delivery for both parcel post and letter-type items is ¥250. For advice of delivery, ask for a form for *uketori tsuuchi*.

Insure anything you're sending overseas. Up to ¥20,000 of insurance for letters and packages costs ¥400, and each additional ¥20,000 or fraction thereof is ¥50 extra.

Unfortunately, insurance, express mail, registered mail, and advice of delivery services are not available to all countries.

Letter-Post

The weight limit for letters and documents is 2kg. Aerogrammes are classified as letters and can be sent anywhere in the world for a uniform rate of ¥80. If you make a mistake on an aerogramme, you can exchange it at the post office for a new one for a ¥10 fee.

Postcards also have a uniform rate for any destination in the world. The charge is ¥60 for surface mail and ¥70 for airmail. Post offices sell pre-stamped international airmail postcards, and should you make a mistake writing one of these, it can be exchanged at your post office for a new one at a ¥5 charge.

You can send small items under 1kg as small packets for lower rates than if you sent them as parcels. You must take the packet to the counter, and you need to explain the contents with a customs label or customs declaration form (available at the window). Some countries limit small packets to 500g, so check at the counter or call the post office information number at the end of this section.

Parcel Post

The maximum weight for international parcel post is 20kg in most cases, but some countries don't handle items over 10kg, and others set their limit at 15kg. The post office has more details, and customs forms for you to fill out.

The size of your parcel is calculated by adding the longest side to the four shorter sides, ie., the length (or whatever side is longer) plus twice the width and twice the depth. The total of these can be no more than 3m in most cases, but a maximum of 2m applies to some destinations. Additionally, the longest side cannot exceed 1.5m in most cases, or 1.05m in others. Again, the post office will have all the details for you.

Even though customs officials will probably open your package somewhere along the way, it's safer to pack things inside your box in a plastic bag or two to give it some degree of protection against water. You never know what might happen.

EMS

EMS is available to about 70 countries and is expanding gradually to more countries. EMS is for sending business documents and general articles. EMS forms and envclopes are available at post offices.

INTELPOST

INTELPOST uses postal networks and fax transmissions for the fastest international mail service possible. About 40 countries around the world are part of the INTELPOST network, and in most cases messages can be delivered the day they are sent. A smaller version, MINI-INTEL, is also available.

INTELPOST rates to participating countries in Asia, Oceania, North America and the Middle East are ¥1,500 for the first page and ¥500 for each additional page. INTELPOST to Europe, South America and Brazil runs ¥2,100 for the first page, and ¥900 per page thereafter.

MINI-INTEL is based on one A5 (14.8cm by 21cm) message space, and can be sent to any participating country for a uniform rate of ¥1,100.

Information

The Central Post Office has numbers you can call for general information about domestic and international postal matters. The services are in Japanese only.

Information (Domestic)   03-3284-9539
                 (International)   03-3284-9540

Air Mail Rates

	zone 1	zone 2	zone 3
Letter (Up to 10g)	¥80	¥100	¥120
Each additional 10g	+¥60	+¥70	+¥100
Postcard	¥70	¥70	¥70
Printed matter and literature			
for the blind (Up to 20g)	¥70	¥80	¥90
Each additional 20g	+¥30	+¥40	+¥50
Small Packet (Up to 80g)	¥160	¥200	¥240
Each additional 20g	+¥30	+¥40	+¥50
Aerogramme	¥80	¥80	¥80

zone 1: Asia

zone 2: North America, Central America, Oceania, Middle East

zone 3: Europe, Africa, South America

What English-Language Daily Newspapers are Available in Japan?

There are four daily English-language newspapers published in Tokyo.

Asahi Evening News - ¥120/copy or ¥3,300/month. The only English-language evening paper in Japan. Answers to the crossword are in the following day's edition. Good attention to Japanese news. Subscription info - 03-3545-0131, ext. 3081.

The Daily Yomiuri - ¥100/copy or ¥2,100/month. The least expensive of the four. Averages about 12 pages, with color photos in some editions. Crossword answers in the next day's copy. If you're a Yomiuri Giants fan, this is the paper for you. Subscription info - 03-3216-8866 or toll free 0120-431-159

The Japan Times - ¥160/copy or ¥4,300/month. The most expensive and the one with the most pages (about 22). Good coverage of international news. Crossword answers in the same issue. Regular column on Japanese baseball! Subscription info - toll free 0120-036-242

Mainichi Daily News - ¥120/copy or ¥3,400/month. Japan's oldest newspaper organization. A little harder to find at train stations, but a good paper. Good coverage of Japanese news. Crossword answers in same issue. Subscription info - 03-3212-3266

Getting a Subscription

You can buy these newspapers by the copy from sales

booths in train stations, or you can subscribe by calling the numbers above. Another way to subscribe is to wait until the newspaper salesmen come around. They're most active at the start of each university semester, when large numbers of students have just moved into new apartments and need newspapers.

Some subscription salesmen will be taken aback when a foreigner opens the door, but some will see you as just another business opportunity and start their hard sell, in Japanese. If you can find out which paper he's from and if it's the one you want, you can get a subscription from him. As a bonus, you'll probably get thank-you gifts of a wash towel or a couple of boxes of laundry soap.

The most common way of paying for a subscription is to wait for the paperboy to come around. (Papergirls are more common than before, but they're still rare.) When you're low on cash and there's a knock at the door, it's usually either the paperboy or the NHK people coming for their due.

How Can I Get Basic Services Turned On and Off?

Electricity

Tokyo Electric Power Company (TEPCO) provides electricity for most of the Tokyo area. Getting the power turned on is pretty easy. Over your front door or in some other out of the way place in your house or apartment is a board with several small switches and one large switch on it. The small switches are circuit breakers, and the large one is, in Japanese, an *ampea bureekaa*, or ampre breaker. When you move in, the ampre breaker should be in the down, or "off" position. All you have to do is push it to the "on" position, and you should have electricity. If you don't have power after you switch the ampre breaker on, make sure the other breakers are also in the "on" position. If that fails, call TEPCO. There will be a postcard addressed to TEPCO attached to the breaker box. Fill it in (ask your landlord or a neighbor if you need help) and drop it in a mailbox. The electric company will transfer the account to your name and start sending the bills.

If your power suddenly goes out, check to see if you've tripped one of the breakers. Drawing more electricity than the breakers can handle will trip one or more of them to the "off" position, cutting your electricity. Turn off a few appliances and reset the breakers to the "on" position. If that doesn't restore your power, call TEPCO.

You can have your electricity bill deducted automatically from your bank account if you sign an agreement with the bank and the utilities company. Most banks offer this service and they have the necessary forms. If you pay your bill this way, the meter-reader will calculate your bill and deduct it from your account in one quick step. If you don't use the automatic transfer system, the meter-reader leaves a copy of your reading in the mailbox, then the electric company mails you a bill which you can pay at banks, (including credit unions), the post office, your local TEPCO office, or at most convenience stores (if your bill has a bar code. See p. 96). If payment for your bill is deducted directly from your account, TEPCO will give you a receipt the next time they read your meter.

To have the service cut off, call the electric company when you have decided your moving day. They'll send a representative to calculate your final bill and to cut off the power. In addition to your name, address and the date you're leaving, they'll want the customer number from your bill or receipt.

TEPCO Information   03-3501-8111

Gas

If you live in or anywhere near the Tokyo area, Tokyo Gas is your gas company. They use two types of gas, 12A and 13A, and appliances differ depending on the type of gas they handle, so always make sure any gas appliance you buy matches the type of gas in your area.

When you move in you need to call Tokyo Gas and have them turn your gas on. If you don't speak Japanese, ask the landlord or a neighbor to call for you. Tokyo Gas will send an official to your home, so you need to arrange a time to meet. The representative will unseal your gas cock, check the gas lines, and look over your gas appliances to make sure they're compatabile with the gas supplied to your area.

You can have your gas bill automatically debited to your account by an automatic transfer, and as with paying your electric bill by this method, the next month's meter reading slip is also your receipt. If you don't pay automatically you still get the meter reading, but your bill will be mailed to you later. You can pay your Tokyo Gas bill at banks or credit associations, post offices, Tokyo Gas offices and most convenience stores if your bill has a bar code on it.

If you're moving out, call Tokyo Gas two or three days before you want the gas shut off. They'll ask your name, address, customer number and the date you're leaving. Like the electric company, the gas company will send somebody out to shut everything off and tally up your final bill.

Tokyo Gas Information   03-3433-2111

Telephone Bills- NTT

Domestic telephone service is billed separately from international service, so expect to get two phone bills if you make overseas calls.

NTT charges a monthly fee of ¥1,550 for private lines, and ¥2,350 for lines used by businesses. Fees for all your outgoing calls are added to this and the total is on your bill.

Your NTT bill comes every month, and is payable at banks, credit associations, post offices, NTT offices and most convenience stores. If you pay by automatic transfer, a receipt for the previous month is mailed to you with the amount to be deducted for the current month.

If you don't pay your bill by the deadline printed on the front, a penalty will be added to your next bill. (Don't panic if the deadline slips past you. You can pay bills even when they are overdue.) Your phone will be disconnected if you don't pay your bill within about three weeks of the deadline.

Telephone Bills- Long Distance Services

IDC, ITJ and KDD all have billing systems similar to NTT's. You can wait for the bills to be mailed to you, then pay them at banks, credit unions and post offices (not many convenience stores handle international telephone bills), or you can sign automatic transfer agreements with the companies involved. You can pay your KDD bill at NTT offices, but not your IDC or ITJ bills.

Water

Water services are not turned off like gas and electricity are, so you don't need to ask the water company to turn your water on. You should, however, call or write the water company and let them know you've moved in so they can switch the account to your name.

Your water meter is checked once every four months, but you're billed every two months. The first bill is based on the water company's estimate of how much water you used, and the second bill is based on the meter reading. The amount you paid for the first bill is adjusted into the second.

Additionally, you're billed for water going into the sewage and drainage system from your home.

Water companies are not organized on as large a scale as the electric and gas companies, and as a result their bills aren't payable in as many places. Banks, credit associations and the post offices can handle them, as well as the local water company's offices, but in most cases convenience stores cannot handle your water bill.

Tokyo Metropolitan Bureau Of Waterworks 03-5320-6327

NHK

NHK is the *Nippon Housou Kyoukai*, or Japan Broadcasting Corporation. They're the people that air some pretty good documentaries, features and specials, as well as some high quality sports and education programs. They're also the people that come around at night and demand money for a contract you never asked for.

NHK is good television, and the rates they charge for the services they provide - two normal stations plus two satellite stations - are reasonable. But why should you pay for something you didn't ask for? Because:

> The Broadcast Law of Japan, enacted in 1950, is applicable to all residents of Japan, regardless of nationality. It provides for two types of broadcasters: the public network NHK... which is supported entirely by receiving fees; and commercial broadcasters.... NHK must depend entirely on the Receiving Fee; it does not broadcast commercials.

No problem with that. But the logic in the next sentence is troublesome.

> So anyone who owns a TV set is required by the Broadcast Law to enter into a Broadcast Receiving Contract with NHK and pay the fee. (From the NHK booklet "To television set owners:")

So, if you own a television set you are required by law to pay about ¥1,320 a month, or about ¥2,250 a month if you have a satellite dish. Do you watch NHK? Do you agree with the views represented on NHK? Do you have any voice in the programming? Did you ask for NHK? Is it worth arguing?

It may take a while after you move in for the NHK people to find you, but they will, and they won't be too troubled by the fact that you're a foreigner. They know you know why they're there.

You can pay your NHK charges directly to the collection people, at banks, credit unions, post offices and most convenience stores, or by automatic transfer.

NHK (toll free)   0120-151-515

What's the Fastest Way to Narita Airport? The Cheapest?

The fastest way to get to Narita Airport depends of course on where you're starting from. On your way to Narita you will most likely pass through Shinjuku, Ueno or some other major station, so the chart below is based on departures from those stations.

From	Transportation	Time Req.	Fare (one-way)
Tokyo	JR Narita Express	53 min.	¥2,890
	Limousine Bus	90 min.	¥2,600
	JR Airport Narita (Sobu-Yokosuka line)	80 min.	¥1,260
Ueno	Keisei Skyliner	61 min.	¥1,740
	Keisei Limited Express	72 min.	¥940
TCAT	Limousine Bus	70 min.	¥2,500
	Taxi	80 min.	over ¥16,000
Shinjuku	JR Narita Express	74 min.	¥3,050
	Limousine Bus	120 min.	¥2,700

A ¥16,000 taxi fare from Narita is often used as an example of how expensive it can be to live in Japan, but it's not a very realistic example. Narita is nowhere near Tokyo, so of course it's expensive. Unless you're really trying to impress somebody there's no need whatsoever to take a taxi.

The Keisei Skyliner is fast and cheap. Reservations are required, but you can usually get them at Keisei Ueno Station if you show up 30 or 40 minutes before you want to leave. The Keisei Limited Express costs about half the

Skyliner's fee and only takes a little longer. Reservations are neither required nor available, and the limited express leaves at 20 minute intervals.

Keisei Ueno Station is a short walk from JR Ueno Station, which can be inconvenient if you have a lot of luggage. For more information about the Skyliner or the Limited Express, call the Keisei Information Line at 03-3831-0131.

The Narita Express (N'EX) is the fastest way to Narita. Reservations are required and spots sell out quickly, so buy your tickets as soon as you know your departure date. Information is available from the JR East Infoline at 03-3423-0111, and you can make reservations at any JR ticketing window. Reservations are not required for the Airport Narita.

Limousine Buses stop at a number of major stations and hotels in the Tokyo area, plus TCAT and the Yokohama City Air Terminal (YCAT). Another point in the service's favor is that you don't have to haul your luggage from this station to that station or down these stairs and up those. Attendants will stow your bags under the bus when you get on, so you don't have to think about them until you've reached Narita.

Reservations are required, but as with the Keisei Skyliner, you can usually get them if you show up at the ticket office 20 minutes before you want to leave. One drawback of bus service is that transit time varies with the traffic conditions. The times listed are fair averages.

Limousine Bus Information   03-3665-7232

I Don't Want to Carry All This Luggage. How Can I Send My Bags to the Airport?

Public transportation to and from Narita Airport is pretty good, but having to haul your luggage all the way from your home can start your trip on the wrong foot. Limousine Buses will stow and haul your bags for you, but there are also several companies that will deliver your suitcases to and from the airport for you.

In general, all you need to do is call one of the companies below a few days before your flight. Give them your name, the date and time of your flight, your flight number, and what airline you'll take. They'll ask for your address and phone number, and set a date to pick up your bags. In most cases you should pay when you get your bags.

Some companies won't pick up your bags on Sundays or holidays, so check before it's too close to your departure date.

They'll give you a claim ticket when they pick up your bags. When you get to Narita, just go to the company's pick up counter and collect your bags. Pick up counters are on the departure floor (4F). Sending your bags is a lot easier than struggling with them all across Tokyo.

None of the delivery companies handle dangerous objects or valuables, but some have packing services for baggage other than suitcases. Ask when you call.

Below are two of the companies that will deliver your luggage to Narita Airport from within the Tokyo area.

Air Baggage Service Company (abc)   03-3545-1131
    They will carry one bag of up to 30 kg for ¥2,060.
    Additional bags ¥1,000 each

Yamato Transport Company   03-3541-3411
    About ¥1,900 per bag, 20kg limit

These companies and others will also deliver your bags <u>from</u> Narita. To have your bags delivered from Narita, go to the delivery company's counter on the arrival floor (1F). The fees for bags from Narita are about the same as for bags to Narita, but the delivery time varies with the season. They'll tell you at the counter how long you can expect to wait. A delivery from Narita to a Tokyo area address typically takes two or three days.

What Kind of Delivery Services Does Japan Have?

In addition to an efficient postal system, Japan has a number of easy to use domestic delivery services. Many convenience stores, liquor stores and other small shops act as pick up spots for delivery companies. The easiest way to tell is to look for a company logo (see below) on a sign in front of the store or in a window.

To send a package from one of these stores, just fill out a delivery form (see below) and give them your package. The store will charge you the delivery fee, and they will keep your package until the delivery company collects it.

The maximum weight for this service is 20kg, and the length, width and height should <u>total</u> less than 120cm, but as long as your package isn't obviously over the limits the convenience store people aren't too strict.

Despite the fact that your package is automatically insured for up to ¥300,000, delivery companies will not transport cash or valuables. They also don't handle animals, dangerous items and things like that. Use common sense.

Your package can get almost anywhere on Honshu, the main island, within two days, and anywhere in Japan in four or five days.

Below are a few of Japan's major delivery companies and the logos to look for.

Yamato Transport (also known as "kuroneko Yamato"- a black cat)

Nippon Express (Pelican Bin)
Seino Transportation (Kangaroo Bin)

Below is a sample shipping order.

Not all companies offer the "special" delivery services below, but each company has something different. The services below are a sample of what's out there.

Ski and Golf Equipment

Carrying skis or golf equipment on the train is about as much fun as, well, carrying your luggage out to Narita Airport. Fortunately, delivery companies have special services that will do the dirty work for you. In most cases the charges for golf or ski transport are a few hundred yen tacked on to the usual fees.

"Cool" Service

Yamato has another special service for sending things

that need to be kept cool or frozen. "Cool Takkyubin" will keep flowers, food, beer and what have you at your choice of 5 °C, 0 °C or –18 °C. Cool.

After Hours Delivery

If you check a blank on the shipping order, the company will deliver your package between 6:00pm and 8:00pm. Without this, the delivery people will wait until the next day to delivery your package, so this service can save some time.

TAKUHAI

5 Saving Money

Where Can I Buy High Quality Used Goods?

Japan seems a bit confused when it comes to used goods. Japanese products are known around the world for their quality and durability, yet every year mountains of perfectly usable goods are thrown away because they are no longer in fashion or the styles have changed. The quest to keep up with the neighbors knows few limits, and the commercial media exploits this to the fullest.

This preference for the newest model is to your advantage, as you can find last year's models at very attractive prices- but you have to look for them. Stores that sell less popular merchandise are naturally less popular with the general public, so their shops are a bit harder to find than the larger department stores. The shops below can be near major stations, like Shinjuku or Ikebukuro, but they're not in the shopping centers and they don't have big ad campaigns or high profiles. They're off on a side street, waiting for you to discover them.

Recycle Shops

Recycle shops are shops that deal in second-hand merchandise. Second-hand doesn't mean a recycle shop's wares are defective or shoddy, but it does mean they sell good quality items for much less than the cost of a top of the line version of the same item.

Household items are the most common items handled by recycle shops, but by no means the only ones. Wardrobes, air conditioners, televisions, washing machines and the like are available in various sizes and styles. Electrical appliances are usually in working condition, and most recycle shops give you a guarantee (and you shouldn't buy one <u>without</u> a guarantee). Most shops will deliver your purchases for a small fee.

Because out-of-fashion items are not popular with most Japanese consumers, you can walk away with useful, practical items at fractions of the cost of the newest models. Why spend ¥300 per load to wash your laundry when you can buy a washing machine for less than ¥6,000?

Shichiya-san

The *shichiya-san* is Japan's pawn shop. The principle of the pawn shop is the same, borrowing money using some of your belongings as collateral, but you're better off not borrowing from the *shichiya*. Instead, you can buy all sorts of interesting and useful items at the pawn shop. Of course, there are always a good number of junk items and the standard collections of watches, cameras and jewelry, but even those can prove interesting. Where else can you find a case of 24 Buddha statuettes for under ¥3,000?

Pawn shops aren't likely to lend money on older items unless they're antiques, so most of their stock is newer than the recycle shops'. For the same reason, newer merchandise at pawn shops is cheaper than at most other outlets, but more expensive than a recycle shop's older merchandise.

When you look for the *shichiya-san*, look for the kanji below.

shichiya   質屋

shichiten 質店

    Below is a small sampling of pawn shops in the central Tokyo area.

<u>Sekine</u>   A discount shop/pawn shop chain with branches in five regions of central Tokyo.

Ikebukuro	West exit (pawn shop)	03-3971-2882
	(discount shop)	03-3983-6147
	East exit (pawn shop)	03-3971-4543
	(discount shop)	03-3981-9823

Shinjuku	(pawn shop)	03-3352-7325
	(discount shop)	03-3225-6504
Shibuya	(pawn/discount shop)	03-3464-2061
Shimbashi	(pawn shop)	03-3504-2070
	(discount shop)	03-3504-2068

Maruichi The Maruichi Group operates two shops in central Tokyo area. They carry a wide variety of merchandise.

Yotsuya-sanchome	On the Marunouchi line.
	03-3355-0777
Otsuka	2 min. from JR Otsuka Station.
	03-3910-0066

Yokoguraya

Tamachi	03-3451-1552
Ebisu	Near the station, behind Sakura Bank
	03-3713-0084
Meguro	Near the station, behind Asahi Bank
	03-3441-8524

Kurata Shichiten

Ikebukuro	03-3988-1023

What Can I Rent in Japan, and Where Can I Rent It?

Tokyo's rental shops handle a variety of items. CD and video rental shops are by far the most common stores, but shops renting tuxedos, suitcases, barbecue grills, and many other items are also available.

CDs and Videos

To rent CDs or videos you need to register with the rental shop first. Most shops don't charge a membership fee, but you need to show your ARC as proof of your address. If there is a membership fee, it's under ¥400 or so. Some rental shops sell insurance, protecting a CD or video against damage as long as you have it out (details vary). The insurance is very cheap, usually around ¥100 a year.

CD and video rental shops often sell blank audio and video tapes, which gives you an idea of the esteem in which copyright laws are held.

Clothing

Formal clothing, especially traditional Japanese formal clothing, can be a huge investment for the average person, to say nothing of someone who only needs a tuxedo or formal dress for one night. Fortunately, Tokyo has many shops that rent kimonos, tuxedos, prom dresses, wedding gowns and other formal wear.

Larger men may have trouble getting clothes with proper leg and sleeve lengths, but if you ask the rental shop far enough in advance they can alter the garment.

Another plus for men is that many shops rent black suits, the Japanese man's uniform for funerals and weddings.

The rental itself is not so difficult, but making the necessary arrangements well ahead of the date of your event is critical.

In addition to formal wear, costume rental is also available. Forget witches and ghosts - this Halloween you can be a samurai, a geisha, or if you have the right body, a sumo wrestler. Tokyo costume shops carry a wide range of period clothing, both Japanese and from other countries. If you look, there's no telling what you can find.

Below is a sample of what's out there.

Tokyo Costume   (Tokyo Isho)   03-3485-2101
> 10:00am to 6:00pm Monday through Saturday. Near Yoyogi-Uehara on the Chiyoda or Odakyu lines.

Ricky Sarani   03-3587-0648
> 10:00am to 7:00pm Tuesday through Friday, 10:00am to 5:00pm on Saturdays. In Roppongi.

City Lady   03-3571-0815
> Daily from 11:00am to 8:00pm. Despite the name, they also handle men's wear. In Ginza, in front of the Ginza 8 Chome bus stop.

Other Rentals

Different stores have different specialties, but the examples below rent a good variety of items. If a store is part of a chain, only a few of the Tokyo area shops are listed. There may be a branch closer to you that's not listed, so call and ask before you go.

Suitcases and video-related rentals are the most common items after office furniture.

Sample rental items and fees? A large (72×53×25cm) suitcase for ten days in the ¥4,400 to ¥6,200 range. A hi-fi video deck for one day runs about ¥7,000, and that home karaoke set you've been waiting to spring on the neighbors can be yours for about ¥7,900 a day. Call some of the shops below to see what they have and how much they want for it. Shop around.

The Minamoto Group

Five branches in the Tokyo area, handling office equipment, suitcases, hair dryers, baby carriages, beds, air conditioners and more. 10:00am to 7:00pm. Closed Wednesdays.

Suginami Branch	03-3391-2900
Setagaya Branch	03-3410-2900
Kunitachi Branch	0425-74-2700

United Rent-all

110 stores nationwide, huge variety, pick-up and delivery available. 9:00am to 7:00pm (some branches until 8:00pm), 7 days a week.

Mejiro Store	03-3794-3431
Nakano Store	03-3360-0110
Funabashi Store	0474-65-0100

Rental Acom

Clothes, golf clubs, you name it, all kinds of variety.

Service Center	03-3350-5741
Shinjuku Branch	03-3350-5081
Ikebukuro Branch	03-3988-2841
Shimbashi Branch	03-3503-1151
Kinshicho Branch	03-3633-6266

Rental shops are happy to do business with you, but don't expect them to speak fluent English. Bring a friend who speaks Japanese if you can. The details of the agreements (how much insurance will you take out on the 100 inch projection tv, how will the pool table be delivered and so on) can be difficult. You may be asked to pay a deposit in some cases.

What are Discount Shops and Where are They?

History

A discount shop (*disukaunto shoppu*) is exactly what its name implies: a store that sells things at prices lower than most other stores.

One type of discount store comes from differences in the American and Japanese concepts of department stores. American department stores are typically chain stores that sell high volumes of a variety of goods at low prices. Their rivals are smaller scale specialty stores, that only stock items within a certain sphere and charge specialty prices.

Japanese department stores resemble their counterparts across the Pacific in that they are large chain stores that offer a variety of merchandise, but Japanese traditions of extreme customer service (for example, the girls who welcome you into department store elevators with a deep bow and perfect politeness) and a more "refined" inventory make the department store a bit expensive. The Japanese consumer's alternatives, including small scale specialty shops, are also expensive.

Discount shops may have emerged when a few marketing types experimented with the idea of trading a bit of the smothering service for lower prices. This is not to say that discount stores have poor service, but a balance was reached and customers can wander shops without people yelling "*IRASSHAIMASE*" at them every few paces.

This type of discount store is found off the beaten path, far from major stations. Land is cheaper there, so they can sell at a discount and still turn a profit. Some stock only one type of merchandise - electrical appliances, for example - and others carry a variety of goods including preserved foods, furniture and other household items. You often can recognize a good discount store of this group by the size of its parking lot.

Discount Areas

Another type of discount shop is the sort found in Akihabara, where scores of electronic shops cluster together to form Electricland. There are so many discount shops in one small region that the term discount area is more appropriate, though the area is made up of small, individually-run shops. Electric goodies are by no means all these shops carry, but they are the specialty.

Akihabara is not the only place for electronics. Shinjuku has several large camera stores that also carry a variety of electronics.

The Kanda-Jimbocho-Ochanomizu area has a long academic tradition, which is why it's bursting with shops for new and used books. The large number of stores for musical instruments and sporting goods explains how students spend their free time. Take Hanzomon, Toei Mita or Toei Shinjuku line to Jimbocho, JR Sobu or Chuo line to Ochanomizu, or the Chiyoda line to Shin-Ochanomizu and just wander the area.

Takadanobaba is another college area, and the area stores are similar to those of the Kanda-Jimbocho-Ochanomizu area. JR Yamanote, Seibu Shinjuku, or Tozai line, or Toden (streetcar) line to Takadanobaba.

The area along the west side of the Yamanote line between Okachimachi and Ueno is the Ameyoko, where you can buy all kinds of goods in the atmosphere of an open-air bazaar. Leather goods and clothing items are the area's specialties, but they are by no means the only things for sale there. Ginza line to Ueno, Uenohirokoji, or Suehirocho, or JR Yamanote to Ueno or Okachimachi.

Your Discount Store

The easiest way to find discount stores in your part of Tokyo is to ask your neighbors. They can recommend shops for the items you want and head you in the right direction. It may be smart to ask for a map, because discount stores are more likely to be on major streets than on train lines. Discount stores are typically hard to get to.

If you'd rather not trouble your neighbors, some discount shops are listed below. The closest stations are also listed, though in some cases "closest" is a very relative term.

Discount Shop Saito   Adachi-ku, Ayase 6-26-18
  Chiyoda line to Ayase   03-3606-2758

Suzuki   Toshima-ku, Nishi Sugamo 4-20-4
  Toei Mita line to Nishi Sugamo   03-3915-4166

Ippudo   Shibuya-ku, Sakuragaoka 2-3
  4 minutes out of the South exit of Shibuya station
               03-3461-8933

Endless   Shinjuku-ku, Sumiyoshi 5-4
  Toei Shinjuku line to Akebonobashi   03-3357-6044

Discount Ueno   Edogawa-ku, Minami Koiwa 7-28-7

JR Sobu line to Koiwa, out the South exit, veer left, past Chiba Bank and across from the Echigoya Pawn Shop

03-3659-7321

Are There Any Flea Markets in Japan?

Japan has open-air markets and trade marts that are held seasonally or with holidays and festivals, as well as a number of flea markets and antique markets that are held on a regular basis. Many of the regular markets are held in conjunction with local *jinja*, or shrines. These are usually on the shrine grounds. Some of the regular markets are below. Some markets are open sunrise to sunset, but smart shoppers know the real prizes are gone before noon.

Nogi Jinja (Nogi Shrine)

The second Sunday of every month, sunrise to sunset. Cancelled if it rains. Chiyoda Line to Nogizaka, exit 1.

Togo Jinja (Togo Shrine)

First and fourth Sundays, sunrise to sunset. Chiyoda line to Meiji-Jingumae, or Yamanote line to Harajuku.

Hanazono Jinja (Hanazono Shrine)

Second and third Sundays, sunrise to sunset. Cancelled if it rains. Marunouchi line or Toei Shinjuku line to Shinjuku-sanchome. Take Meiji-dori about two blocks past Yasukuni-dori, then turn left. Or ask someone.

Iidabashi Antique Market

The first Saturday of every month, sunrise to sunset. Yurakucho line, Tozai line or JR Sobu line to Iidabashi. Central Plaza Building, near JR Iidabashi station.

Salvation Army Bazaar

Every Saturday, but only until 12:30pm. Take bus #19 from the West exit of Shinjuku station (for Gissho Koseikai Seido) to Boshibyo-mae (see p. 68 for bus riding techniques)   03-3384-3769

Arai Yakushi

The first Sunday of every month, sunrise to sunset. Cancelled if it rains. Seibu Shinjuku line to Arai Yakushi-mae station.

Aoyama Antique Market

The third Saturday of every month, sunrise to sunset. Ginza line to Gaien-mae. CI Plaza.

Roppongi

The fourth Thursday and Friday of every month, roughly sunrise to sunset. In front of the Roppongi Roi Building. East down Gaien Higashi Dori, across from Sakura Bank.

Recycle Undo Shimin no Kai and the Nippon Recycle Undo Shimin no Kai usually hold markets once a month, but the sites vary from month to month. For more information, call Recycle Undo Shimin no Kai at 03-3226-6800, or Nippon Recycle Undo Shimin no Kai at 03-5228-3300 or 03-5228-3305.

How Else Can I Buy Things at Low Prices?

Networking

The best deals you find will come from friends or acquaintences returning to their home countries. They can't or don't want to take everything back with them, and they won't throw something away when they can make some money, no matter how little.

Household items are the most common goods returnees will part with, but by no means the only ones. It's cheaper to buy tableware, utensils, pots and pans all over again than to ship them home, so these can be found at bargain prices. Furniture is also expensive to ship overseas, which means you can find this at good deals as well.

What is the best way to get in on these deals? Keep in touch with your friends and acquaintances. When they make their decisions about what will stay and what will go, let them know what you're interested in. Act fast, because the best items sell quickly.

Networking is communicating. Even if none of your friends or acquaintances are moving, they may know someone or someone who knows someone who has what you want and might consider a sale. Networking often seems a lost art, but you can save some money if you communicate your wants and listen to what is available to you.

Buying from foreigners other than your friends and acquaintances can also save you money, but you need to keep your eyes and ears open. The Monday issue of the Daily Yomiuri, for example, features a section of classified ads full of people selling things they don't need, don't want, or just can't keep anymore. A sample of items includes telephone lines in the ¥65,000 range, several different types of cameras and fax machines, household goods (hair dryer, ¥3,000) and other used items.

Bulletin boards are another way to track down bargains. Notices at your workplace are often the most helpful, but you can also find good information on your city or ward notice boards, as well as your neighborhood announcement boards. Notice boards at local colleges or universities have particularly good leads around the end of the school year, when students graduate and move on.

Most sales of this sort are on a no-returns basis. But how can you return something to someone who's left the country already?

What Services are Available to Me? What Does My Local Government Provide?

A number of advice, counseling, therapy, information and other services are available to foreigners living in the Tokyo area.

TELL (Tokyo English Life Line)   03-5481-4347
> A crisis management and counseling hotline. They offer advice, help and referrals. 9:00am to 4:00pm and 7:00pm to 11:00pm everyday.

The Japan Helpline   0120-46-1997
> Counseling and information 24 hours a day, toll free.

Agape House   0120-46-1996
> Counseling and help with cross-cultural difficulties. Toll free, 24 hours a day.

HELP Asian Women's Shelter   03-3368-8855
> A crisis and help line for Asian women. Counseling in English, Japanese and other languages. Weekdays, 9:30am to 5:30pm. (Emergency calls accepted 24 hours)

The Tokyo Metropolitan Government   03-5320-7744
Foreign Residents' Advisory Center
> Advice and information on a wide range of topics. English assistance is available at the above number from 9:30am to noon, 1:00pm to 4:00pm Monday through Friday. Advice in other languages is also available. (See p. 74 for more information.)

Alcoholics Anonymous 03-3971-1471
  Many meetings throughout Tokyo.

Counseling International 03-3408-0496
  Family, marriage and individual counseling and therapy.

Your ward and city offices offer a variety of counseling and information services at no cost to you. Unfortunately many of these programs are only in Japanese, so you may need a friend to help you.

A partial listing of services offered by Edogawa Ward, for example, includes counseling and information on raising children, education issues, labor and tenant's rights, and consumer matters.

Local governments also hold a variety of educational meetings and classes. These are usually limited to people living or working within the ward. Chiyoda Ward and Chofu City, for example, sponsor Japanese classes (see p. 56). Check with your city or ward office to find out exactly what programs are available.

Your ward or city also has a number of special facilities for you to use. Again, these are often limited to residents of the city or ward. Local governments provide you with public libraries, gyms, meeting halls, museums, parks and sports grounds. Central libraries are more likely than branch libraries to have English and other foreign language books, but you won't know until you check.

Some wards open their facilities to the general public, and many public sports centers have services and equipment to match private sports clubs. Public gyms and sports centers are far easier on your budget. Some are listed below.

Tokyo Taiikukan   03-5474-2111

> A good fitness gym and a good location. 9:30am to 8:00pm. JR Sobu line to Sendagaya, 1 min.

Minato Kuritsu Sports Center   03-3452-4151

> Gym, weight and exercise room, indoor pool and other facilities. Tennis courts are restricted to ward residents and workers. Ward residents and workers only on the first and third Sundays. Closed Mondays. 9:00am to 9:00pm. JR to Tamachi station, 4 min.

Katsushika Kuritsu Sogo Sports Center   03-3691-7111

> Training room, gym, archery range, running track, indoor and outdoor pools and others. The catch is, it's not easy to get to. JR Sobu line to Shin Koiwa, then Keisei Bus to Kameyari via Shiratori. Get off at the Okudo 3 Chome bus stop. 9:00am to 9:00pm.

Similar to the custom of taking off your shoes at the door of a Japanese home, many gyms and sports centers expect you to have a pair of "indoor" shoes for gym use. Bring your own towel and other items.

Most cities and wards operate swimming pools and the same residents-and-workers-only rule may or may not apply. Check before you go. Public swimming pools are much cheaper than private pools, but also more crowded, especially in the heat of a Tokyo summer. Many pools require swimming caps.

Where Can I Find a Good, Inexpensive Meal?

Lunch is one of Japan's best food bargains. The most common bargain lunch is the set menu, or *teishoku*. The content of these sets varies from shop to shop, but *teishoku* usually cost in the ¥900 to ¥1,200 range. Even more expensive restaurants loosen up and offer affordable *teishoku* for the lunch crowd.

Food is always above or below you in a Japanese department store. Most department stores have restaurants or coffee shops on their top floors, and supermarkets in the basements. The restaurants will have inexpensive *teishoku*, and even after lunch they can offer cheaper meals than other places. However, the more expensive and upscale the department store is, the more expensive and upscale the restaurants in it are.

Larger Japanese supermarkets serve a variety of dishes at very reasonable prices. For example, various types of *yakitori* sell for as little as ¥80 a stick, and you can find *takikomi-gohan* or *sansai-gohan* (rice dishes with lots of other goodies thrown in) for around ¥300 per 100g. Every supermarket's repertoire is different, so see what your local stores offer. You can sample a number of different Japanese dishes at your supermarket.

In addition to prepared foods, many supermarkets also have tiny restaurants tucked away in their back corners. These are usually inexpensive, and they often specialize in one type of dish.

Another way to save at your supermarket is to check your calendar. Most stores close for one day during the week. Rather than open up after the holiday with shelves full of spoiled meat, fish and other items, many supermarkets have big sales on perishables the evening before their holiday. If you mark your calendar or remember the holiday schedule, you can save 30 to 70 percent on your grocery shopping, depending on the item and how close it is to closing time.

Chinese restaurants, curry rice shops, shops for *gyuudon* (slices of beef on a bowl of rice) or for *soba* and *raamen* ("noodles and soup" is a crude description, but it's accurate enough), are inexpensive, reliable standbys. Most neighborhoods have at least one of these shops. Yoshinoya and Matsuya are two popular chains for *gyuudon*. Stand-up soba and *raamen* shops, where you eat standing at the counter, are quick and inexpensive.

Busier train stations usually have small restaurants, but sometimes these are as expensive as regular restaurants. Look for a menu or price list before you commit yourself.

For a cheap bite of your favorite sushi, try *kaitenzushi*. You can recognize these shops by the "sushi-go-round" conveyor belt that carries plates of sushi around the counter. *Kaitenzushi* shops are based on self-service. Sit down at the counter and take a mug from the rack above the conveyor. Usually there's a green tea bag in it, so just fill the mug with hot water from a tap near the counter for your tea. (Other drinks are available, but tea is free.) Next, wait for your favorite sushi to come by on the conveyor. Take what you want, leave what you don't, and ask for anything that's not on the belt.

The color or type of plate the sushi is on shows how much it costs, so you can keep track of your bill by matching the dishes you've emptied with a price chart on the wall. A plate of two pieces of sushi costs from ¥100 to ¥300, depending on the type.

Izakaya fall in the gray areas between taverns, bars and restaurants. Food and beer or other drinks are usually more reasonable at *izakaya* than at bars or other establishments, and the atmosphere is comfortable and *genki*. These are lively places to eat and drink with friends.

Some *izakaya* are operated by individuals and some are run as chains, but in both cases you can recognize them by their signs- they use a <u>lot</u> of red - and there's often a red paper lantern out in front of the shop.

An irregular sort of restaurant is the *yatai*, the portable stand that sets up on streetcorners and sidewalks. *Yatai* serve *yakisoba*, boiled foods (*oden*) and other goodies. Prices for food and drinks are very reasonable, even if there's not a lot of variety. The atmosphere is very casual and relaxed- it's hard to be stiff and formal when you're eating in a little stall in the street.

Other Info

Japanese

Japanese uses two scripts, hiragana and katakana, in addition to *kanji*, Chinese characters. Katakana is most often used for foreigners' names, as well as foreign words and ideas. It is also used to call attention to a word.

Katakana

ア	イ	ウ	エ	オ		ハ	ヒ	フ	ヘ	ホ
a	i	u	e	o		ha	hi	fu	he	ho
カ	キ	ク	ケ	コ		マ	ミ	ム	メ	モ
ka	ki	ku	ke	ko		ma	mi	mu	me	mo
サ	シ	ス	セ	ソ		ヤ		ユ		ヨ
sa	shi	su	se	so		ya		yu		yo
タ	チ	ツ	テ	ト		ラ	リ	ル	レ	ロ
ta	chi	tsu	te	to		ra	ri	ru	re	ro
ナ	ニ	ヌ	ネ	ノ		ワ		ヲ		ン
na	ni	nu	ne	no		wa		wo		n

Hiragana

あ	い	う	え	お		た	ち	つ	て	と
a	i	u	e	o		ta	chi	tsu	te	to
か	き	く	け	こ		な	に	ぬ	ね	の
ka	ki	ku	ke	ko		na	ni	nu	ne	no
さ	し	す	せ	そ		は	ひ	ふ	へ	ほ
sa	shi	su	se	so		ha	hi	fu	he	ho

ま	み	む	め	も		ら	り	る	れ	ろ
ma	mi	mu	me	mo		ra	ri	ru	re	ro

や		ゆ		よ		わ		を		ん
ya		yu		yo		wa		wo		n

Other sounds are formed by adding notations to the bases above.

Katakana

ガ	ギ	グ	ゲ	ゴ		バ	ビ	ブ	ベ	ボ
ga	gi	gu	ge	go		ba	bi	bu	be	bo

ザ	ジ	ズ	ゼ	ゾ		パ	ピ	プ	ペ	ポ
za	ji	zu	ze	zo		pa	pi	pu	pe	po

ダ	ヂ	ヅ	デ	ド
da	ji	zu	de	do

Hiragana

が	ぎ	ぐ	げ	ご		ば	び	ぶ	べ	ぼ
ga	gi	gu	ge	go		ba	bi	bu	be	bo

ざ	じ	ず	ぜ	ぞ		ぱ	ぴ	ぷ	ぺ	ぽ
za	ji	zu	ze	zo		pa	pi	pu	pe	po

だ	ぢ	づ	で	ど
da	ji	zu	de	do

Helpful Addresses and Telephone Numbers

*Police (Emergencies) 110
  Information 03-3501-0110
  Lost and Found 03-3814-4151
*Hospitals (Emergencies) 119
  Information 03-3212-2323
*Subway Information (Eidan) 03-3837-7111
*JR East Infoline 03-3423-0111
*Narita Flight Information 0476-32-2800
*Foreign Residents' Advisory Center 03-5320-7744
*Japan Helpline 0120-46-1997
*Tokyo Regional Tax Bureau 03-3216-6811
*NTT Information 03-3277-1010
*KDD Information 0057
*ITJ Information 0120-440-041
*IDC Information 0120-030-061
*Post Office Information (Domestic) 03-3284-9539
  (International) 03-3284-9540
*Tokyo Gas Information 03-3433-2111
*NHK 0120-151-515
*TELL (Tokyo English Life Line) 03-5481-4347
*Agape House 0120-46-1996
*HELP Asian Women's Shelter 03-3368-8855
*Alcoholics Anonymous 03-3971-1471

Embassies and Consulates in Tokyo
Australia
  03-5232-4111
  2-1-14 Mita, Minato-ku 108
Canada
  03-3408-2101
  7-3-38 Akasaka, Minato-ku 107
France
  03-5420-8800
  4-11-44 Minami-Azabu, Minato-ku 106
Germany
  03-3473-0151

4-5-10 Minami-Azabu, Minato-ku 106
India
  03-3262-2391
  2-2-11 Kudan Minami, Chiyoda-ku 102
Ireland
  03-3263-0695
  Kowa 25 Bldg., 8-7 Sanbancho Chiyoda-ku 102
Italy
  03-3453-5291
  2-5-4 Mita, Minato-ku 108
Korea
  03-3452-7611
  1-2-5 Minami-Azabu, Minato-ku 106
New Zealand
  03-3467-2271
  20-40 Kamiyamacho, Shibuya-ku 150
U.K.
  03-3265-5511
  1 Ichibancho, Chiyoda-ku 102
U.S.A.
  03-3224-5000
  1-10-5 Akasaka, Minato-ku 107

Japanese Government Offices

Give'em a call or drop'em a line. Let'em know what you think.
*Imperial Household Agency
  03-3213-1111
  1-1 Chiyoda, Chiyoda-ku 100
*Prime Minister's Office
  03-3581-2361
  1-6 Nagatacho, Chiyoda-ku 100
*Prime Minister's Official Residence
  03-3581-0101
  2-3-1 Nagatacho, Chiyoda-ku 100
*House Of Councillors
  03-3581-3111
  2-1-1 Nagatacho, Chiyoda-ku 100

*House of Representatives
  03-3581-5111
  2-1-2 Nagatacho, Chiyoda-ku 100
*Tokyo Metropolitan Government
  03-5321-1111
  2-8-1 Nishi-Shinjuku, Shinjuku-ku 163-01
*Tokyo Metropolitan Health Department
  03-5320-4485
*Tokyo Metropolitan Bureau of Waterworks
  03-5320-6327

Ward Offices

*Adachi-ku
  03-3882-1111
  1-4-18 Senju, Adachi-ku 120
*Arakawa-ku
  03-3802-3111
  2-2-3 Arakawa, Arakawa-ku 116
*Bunkyo-ku
  03-3812-7111
  1-16-21 Kasuga, Bunkyo-ku 112
*Chiyoda-ku
  03-3264-0151
  1-6-11 Kudan-Minami, Chiyoda-ku 102
*Chuo-ku
  03-3543-0211
  1-1-1 Tsukiji, Chuo-ku 104
*Edogawa-ku
  03-3652-1151
  1-4-1 Chuo, Edogawa-ku 132
*Itabashi-ku
  03-3964-1111
  2-66-1 Itabashi, Itabashi-ku 173
*Katsushika-ku
  03-3695-1111
  5-13-1 Tateishi, Katsushika-ku 124
*Kita-ku
  03-3908-1111
  1-15-22 Oji Honcho, Kita-ku 114

*Koto-ku
  03-3647-9111
  4-11-28 Toyo, Koto-ku 135
*Meguro-ku
  03-3715-1111
  2-4-5 Chuocho, Meguro-ku 152
*Minato-ku
  03-3578-2111
  1-5-25 Shiba-koen, Minato-ku 105
*Nerima-ku
  03-3993-1111
  6-12-1 Toyotama-Kita, Nerima-ku 176
*Nakano-ku
  03-3389-1111
  4-8-1 Nakano, Nakano-ku 164
*Ota-ku
  03-3773-5111
  2-10-1 Chuo, Ota-ku 143
*Setagaya-ku
  03-3412-1111
  4-21-27 Setagaya, Setagaya-ku 154
*Shibuya-ku
  03-3463-1211
  1-1 Udagawacho, Shibuya-ku 150
*Shinagawa-ku
  03-3777-1111
  2-1-36 Hiromachi, Shinagawa-ku 140
*Shinjuku-ku
  03-3209-1111
  1-4-1 Kabukicho, Shinjuku-ku 160
*Suginami-ku
  03-3312-2111
  1-15-1 Asagaya-Minami, Suginami-ku 166
*Sumida-ku
  03-5608-1111
  1-23-20 Azumabashi, Sumida-ku 130
*Taito-ku
  03-5246-1111
  4-5-6 Higashi-Ueno, Taito-ku 110

*Toshima-ku
  03-3981-1111
  1-18-1 Higashi-Ikebukuro, Toshima-ku 170

City Offices

*Akigawa-shi 0425-58-1111
*Akishima-shi 0425-44-5111
*Chofu-shi 0424-81-7111
*Fuchu-shi 0423-64-4111
*Fussa-shi 0425-51-1511
*Hachioji-shi 0426-26-3111
*Higashi-Kurume-shi 0424-73-5111
*Higashi-Murayama-shi 0423-93-5111
*Higashi-Yamato-shi 0425-63-2111
*Hino-shi 0425-85-1111
*Hoya-shi 0424-21-2525
*Inagi-shi 0423-78-2111
*Itsukaichi-shi 0425-96-1511
*Kiyose-shi 0424-92-5111
*Kodaira-shi 0423-41-1211
*Koganei-shi 0423-83-1111
*Kokubunji-shi 0423-25-0111
*Komae-shi 03-3430-1111
*Kunitachi-shi 0425-76-2111
*Machida-shi 0427-22-3111
*Mitaka-shi 0422-45-1151
*Musashi-Murayama-shi 0425-65-1111
*Musashino-shi 0422-51-5131
*Ome-shi 0428-22-1111
*Tachikawa-shi 0425-23-2111
*Tama-shi 0423-75-8111
*Tanashi-shi 0424-64-1311